"From Me, to You..."

a Memoir

Tanika,

Thank you for the love and support soror. I really look forward to your comments.

Love you

"From Me, to You..."

a Memoir

by Phillip Mozelle Black

Written by Phillip M. Black

Edited by Tara L. Washington

Published by Phillip M. Black

ISBN–10: 0-615-31186-5

ISBN-13: 978-0-615-31186-9

Before you read…

From Me, to You is a memoir written in the form of letters to the many people who have influenced my life over the years. Most of the individuals I have written about are from my immediate family on my mother's side; others are either close friends, prominent speakers, writers and even well known musicians. Every situation, concept, or memory revealed in these letters have affected and influenced my life in a myriad of ways. Please note, while the names of the characters have been changed, the stories are all true. These experiences have assisted in molding me into the man that I am today. To my readers; thank you for allowing yourself to become familiar with me, my struggles, and my experiences in life. It is my goal to inspire you all by way of these letters, and provide a source of insight to help you through your journey in life. I dedicate this book to my loving mother Muriel Cornella Black. You have inspired me to be the best that I can in all that I do. Thank you for seeing more inside of me than I ever saw within myself.

Forward

Writing this book was without a doubt, the most difficult task I have ever faced in my entire life. Until now I have hid my inner most thoughts, buried the questions of my heart, and smothered the tears from my soul. This is a project I have locked away in my mind for years. I always knew the Lord would call me to give my testimony; yet I ran from it over and over again. My best friend and I have shared an analogy over the years where I describe my reluctance to take up my calling by saying, "I feel as if I have been getting dressed for the prom and now I am too afraid to go." In spite of my fears I felt in my spirit the time had finally come for me to take up this calling in January of 2009; yet for months I could not come up with a single chapter. In fact, I was not even able to think of a title or decide on a clear direction.

On June 19th, 2009, I was laid off from work. My company closed down the division I over saw as a District Manager. Prior to that day, my original goal was to have the book completed by January of 2010. I only had fifteen pages of random notes accumulated and still no title or focus. Seventeen days later on July 7th, I completed my first draft. Until now, I had feared completing this book. I have always fully understood and saw with clarity the responsibility on my life to bring my journey to the forefront. Before this day, I only allowed people to see the part of me I felt they wanted. Never have I truly let anyone inside my mind, my heart or my soul, the way I have through writing these letters.

It was a tremendous struggle for me to even complete this project. Often times I would have to stop typing due to an unexpected downpour of tears and heightened emotions. I would gather myself, and then come back minutes, hours, even a day or two later to complete my thoughts; sometimes, for just a single paragraph. Everything that has made me who I am is in this book. Those who know me today only hear or read the words I use to inspire. Now you will be introduced to not only my sources of inspiration, but the often lonely and refining road I had to travel in order to gain knowledge and insight.

After reading these letters, those of you whom I have never met may feel you have known me all along. Those of you, who know me well, may feel like you have never really known me at all. If we met through football, you will realize I am more than a jock. If you know me by my artwork, you will recognize I am more than an empty canvas. If you know me through my comedic nature, you will find I am more than just a laugh. If you were drawn to me because of my knowledge of the Word, I am more than a quoted scripture. If you know me through my fraternity, you will see I am more than just a march. For those who have ever heard me sing, I am more than just a note.

Trial after trial, challenge after challenge and disappointment after disappointment has silenced me for over 27 years. But today you will finally here my voice. My true voice.

I am... Phillip Mozelle Black, and this is my story.

Table of Contents

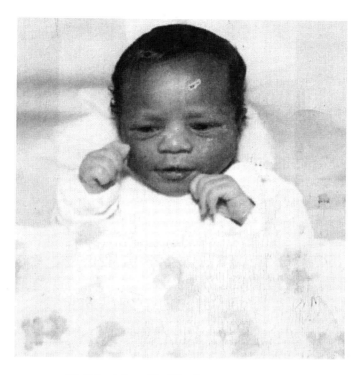

Phillip Mozelle Black June 3, 1977

Preface

Hello,

Let me formally introduce myself. My name is Phillip Mozelle Black. I was born in the heart of Detroit Michigan, June 3, 1977. My family traces its roots back to Louisiana by way of Mississippi. After relocating north to Indianapolis in 1972, my grandmother, with her children moved a second time to Detroit in 1974. After I was born, we only lived in the actual city of Detroit for about six and a half years. From there we moved to Highland Park Michigan. That is where I truly grew up.

Unless you have been to Highland Park, you would not have a single clue as to where to find it on the map. Highland Park – better known as HP - by definition, is a Suburb of Detroit. But if you were to ride through it (especially today), "suburb" would be last word that came to mind. Yet to be from HP, is to love HP. Something I also developed over time growing up there.

Like many people today, I am the product of a single parent home. I was raised by my mother with a little help here and there from my four uncles, two aunts and grandmother. Oh, my dad? Well that's a story all by itself. But I'll share it with you a little later. To give you an idea, I can count on my hands the amount of times I had a chance to see him throughout my entire life. Do not feel too bad for me though. I was still blessed enough to have a mother who loves me to no end. I also had and still have friends and family who more than take up the slack. But, we will talk more about that later. Trust me, I have plenty of sob stories to tell, there is no rush to get into any of them. Besides, I have learned the power of my experiences and how they have helped me grow.

Today, I am at a really good place in my life. I am happier with myself than I have ever been. I am more confident in who I am… why I am… and who I belong to. While that may seem elementary to you, for me it is a major accomplishment, especially considering the long road of self hatred and low self esteem I have traveled. I have always been very self conscious. Whether it was worrying about how I was dressed, the words that I spoke and how they were perceived, or mainly because of my dark complexion.

I was teased a lot as a child. I have heard enough "you so black jokes" to do an all day comedic marathon without repeating one line. One of my favorites, "Boy you so black, when you go swimming it look like a damn oil spill", or, "You so black, you sweat Coffee." Joke after joke, the image being described to me was one of an ugly little black boy who would sweat all the time. One would think things might change for the better as an adult. But it carried on over the years.

They say that kids are cruel but adults can be - and in many cases are - much worse. To a child discretion is close to unknown and honesty reigns. Children are bold, yet are secure enough with so much innocence, that they are able to tell you how they feel face to face. As we grow into adulthood our abilities to mask our true selves and feelings toward one another are enhanced. I have come to respect and appreciate the person that can stand face to face… look me right in the eyes… and say with confidence… "You black as hell." Because I know that person is joking and laughing with me and not at me. As of now, I think I tell more jokes about myself being dark, than anyone else.

The major difference is my understanding of how people tend to point out faults in others because they are unhappy with some part of themselves. I have also learned how to verbally defend myself and release the guilt from my past, by talking about what has occurred. Oh, not to mention dark skinned men are in style thanks to guys like Wesley Snipes, MJ, Djimon Housou, Taye Diggs, Tyrese and Morris Chestnut. Those dudes put us on the map. Besides that - if you can believe it - I am glad for the experience.

I truly feel if I had not been humbled to the degree in which I was early in life, I may not have developed this mentality and philosophy I am sharing with you today. A lot of good came out of my trials. I started playing and developed a love for football and sports in general. I met some great people; teachers, mentors and coaches who not only taught me about math, science and the game, but also about life. Through those life lessons and excelling on the football field, it created the opportunity for me to go to college, meet a host of new people, and grow as a man both personally and professionally.

My life has been filled with good, great and not so happy moments. For a while, it seemed like the less than happy days were the most frequent. As if the only times I had were bad times. Have you ever felt that way before?

Have you ever come to a place in your life where you just got tired? A time when you felt as if you were in the middle of a hurricane filled with dying friends or family, high debt, low money, back bills, bad relationships, poor grades, no gas, Noodles, and one more call off from getting fired? Have you ever been tired like that? Or how about tired to the point of just giving up? And I do not mean quitting your job. I mean when you are at the end of your rope with just enough slack to tie a noose. Thinking to yourself, "I truly feel in the core of my soul, the next bad phone call is going to be the one that makes me hang… it up". I don't know about you, but I have been that tired. How did I get past it? Faith.

It is amazing what happens when all you have left is God. You begin to see people and situations for what they truly are. Hard times have a tendency to bring you to your knees; either in pain or in prayer. But as I continued to fight through the pain, disappointment, heart ache, and loss; I began to recognize just how broad He has made my shoulders through prayer. I learned the old statement is true, "God does not put more on you than you can bear."

This is why I have decided to take a leap of faith and share with you intimate details of my life. I understand the spiritual shoulders I have are wider than the average person. I realize the weight I have been called to lift is not always my own. So my hope is by reading about the many challenges I have faced and overcome; you will receive revelation, knowledge and inspiration to continue your own journey. And instead of tying a noose, you will simply tie a knot and keep holding on.

This is From Me, to You…

If

If you can keep your head when all about you
Are losing theirs and blaming it on you;
If you can trust yourself when all men doubt you,
But make allowance for their doubting too;
If you can wait and not be tired by waiting,
Or, being lied about, don't deal in lies,
Or, being hated, don't give way to hating,
And yet don't look too good, nor talk too wise;

If you can dream - and not make dreams your master;
If you can think - and not make thoughts your aim;
If you can meet with triumph and disaster
And treat those two imposters just the same;
If you can bear to hear the truth you've spoken
Twisted by knaves to make a trap for fools,
Or watch the things you gave your life to broken,
And stoop and build 'em up with wornout tools;

If you can make one heap of all your winnings
And risk it on one turn of pitch-and-toss,
And lose, and start again at your beginnings
And never breath a word about your loss;
If you can force your heart and nerve and sinew
To serve your turn long after they are gone,
And so hold on when there is nothing in you
Except the Will which says to them: "Hold on";

If you can talk with crowds and keep your virtue,
Or walk with kings - nor lose the common touch;
If neither foes nor loving friends can hurt you;
If all men count with you, but none too much;
If you can fill the unforgiving minute
With sixty seconds' worth of distance run -
Yours is the Earth and everything that's in it,
And - which is more - you'll be a Man my son!

Rudyard Kiplin

From Me, to You…

"But the Lord said to Ananias, "Go! This man is my chosen instrument to carry my name before the Gentiles and their kings and before the people of Israel. I will show him how much he must suffer for my name."–Acts 9:15-16

Dear Uncle John,

How have you been? I know we haven't talked much. A lot of our conversations have come about only when we catch up at Uncle Bobby's for the holidays or when we get together to watch a game. I know it's because of me, so I will start calling more and answering the phone. But I'm not writing you to talk about that. There is something else I have always wanted to tell you, I just never knew how. It wasn't until almost two years ago that I even got the courage to share this story with Momma. Like I told her, I want you to know first and foremost, I love you. Nothing can ever change that, not now… not ever. But before I share a part of my past with you, I ask that you will not channel your feelings through anger or confrontation; no matter what. I am only calling it to your attention because I realize how much it helped, when I told Momma, and I think you should know as well. If you continue to read past this point I am assuming (God being our witness) you have agreed to keep it as a conversation.

I'm sure you remember how you use to come pick me and Joel up to take us to places like the park. We use to have a lot of fun. Joel and I would get on the swings, the monkey bars and even the 'Playscape'. You came and got us every now and again for a while. But when you started dating Sandra it became more frequent. Joel and I appreciated it. We enjoyed playing together and having other kids around made it even better. Back then, you and Sandra were so close, and we visited so often, you both began to acknowledge her three kids, along with Joel and me, as cousins. We didn't mind. As a matter of fact we felt the same way. We were always over there. For a while it seemed like almost every weekend. I really liked going over to Sandra's house. Even Sandra's girls were fun to play with and on top of that, T had an Atari. We would play the game all day if you let us. Most of the time Sandra would make us go outside to play at some point....*"Cut that game off and go outside... Ya'll been on that thing forever... Gone mess my TV up."* We use to hear that all the time. I wonder why you adults seemed to think that the game system caused the television to go bad. I guess you all forgot the tv was bad to begin with. But playing inside back then was just as much fun as playing outdoors.

I remember how we all would walk to the park and play until the sun went down during the summer. We played, and played, and played. But one thing was for sure, we knew to be home before the street lights came on. And if anyone forgot, T made sure to remind us. Even though he was older, T didn't seem to mind playing and looking after us. He and I became good friends. I really liked talking to him and playing his video game.

I'll never forget one weekend we stayed over, T and I had to have played tennis on the Atari until at least four in the morning. Not that I was good at telling time yet, after all, I was only five. I just knew it was late. The only reason we turned it off was because Sandra came into the living room and made us...*"Ya'll kids carry ya'll butts to bed! I'm mad I brought that dang'on game!"* Although I had fun playing the game, going to the park with the other kids and getting ice cream; what makes that weekend unforgettable can not even co-exist with the joys of having innocent fun as a child.

16

From Me, to You...

'The next day I think you and Sandra went to the grocery store really early in the morning to get us some breakfast food. You guys must have stopped a few other places because you were gone for a while. So long that we all got out of the bed and dressed ourselves for the day. We did go outside while you were gone. But you said it was ok as long as T was looking after us. And like I said, he never seemed to mind doing just that.'

'After playing catch for a while I had to go potty. I ran back into the house so I wouldn't pee-pee on myself. I had to use the bathroom upstairs because the one downstairs didn't work. When I came out T was in you and Sandra's bedroom.'

"Phillip..."
"Huh?"
"Come here..."
"kay."

When I walked in he was sitting on the edge of the bed. The shades were all closed and the lights were out. I could still see because some of the light forced its way through the top and bottom of the drapes. He had a funny look on his face. He was smiling a bit but his eyes looked strange. Almost like he was looking through me, and not at me.

"Come here", he said, as he gestured for me to come over and sit beside him. I didn't think anything was wrong so I did. Besides, 'this is T, he watches me all the time.'

"You in kindergarten aint you?"

"UnHuh..."

"You got a girl friend?"

"Yeah, I got a lot of girl friends..."

"How many you got?"

"21!"

"Yeah right! Name um..."

"Erica, Keisha, Toya..."

"Okay, Okay.... Well, what do you do with 'um?"

"I-on-know? We play at school..."

"That's all?"

"Yeah! I'mma-go outside..."

"No! Wait a minute..."

"Don't you want to see what they gone look like?"

"I-own-know?"

"Hear, look at this book..."

"Dats-nasty!"

"No it aint... you gone like it when you get older..."

"Un-Uuuun..."

"Yes you will... I bet."

"I'mma-go outside..."

"No, wait… I'm gone show you what to do when you get older…"

"what?"

"Come here…"

"You better not tell nobody. If you do, I aint gone be yo' friend no more. If you tell yo' Momma or yo' Uncle John they not gone like you no more either."

'So I never told anyone. All I could imagine was you or Momma beating my butt and calling me a story teller, or worse, doing something to T, making him not want to be my friend anymore. After all, he had Atari and he was my friend.'

I know you probably couldn't tell, but when you took me to visit him after I first moved back from Florida a few years ago, it took every ounce of me not to put my hands on him. What pissed me off the most was how he tried to talk to me as if we were family for real. Like we were really long lost cousin's reuniting after years of unwanted separation. I visualized myself beating him to death as we stood in the middle of the street. You couldn't see it, but I was crying inside. I felt like that 'little boy' all over again. How could someone take advantage of a child like that? Then leave them with a life of shame, humiliation and questions that may never be answered. But in the midst of that moment of rage, in my spirit I heard the words… "Peace be still." That is the only reason why he is still here today.

I want to remind you of the promise you made to me in the beginning of this letter. My point in telling you this is not because I want anything done; I just needed to talk about it. Revealing this to you has taken years of shame, hurt and guilt out of my life. When I got the courage to tell Momma I felt liberated. I know I didn't do anything wrong. One may question why I chose not to take revenge and what has changed between the time we were standing in front of the house in the street and now?…Not only has my peace returned to me, but I have forgiven him. So I want you to as well. Not because he has a sickness and needs help, but because it had to happen. That moment in my life had to occur. That experience in my life and my struggle through that journey had to take place. I have revealed and I am healing, and I now understand that revealing is ok. It is ok to tell someone. It is ok to talk about it. I had to experience the shame and fear, and overcome in order to tell anyone else that has gone through the same thing that it is and will be okay. You did nothing wrong. And yes… God does love you.

Uncle John this may not need to be said but I will say it anyway… I don't fault you, Momma or anyone else. I truly don't. In fact, the reason God chose to keep me mute about it all of these years, is because He knew then exactly what I know now. You or Momma would have gone to jail. I know you both love me and would have protected me. I love you Unc. And if you pass this letter to T, tell him, "repent and your sins will be forgiven."

Love you,

Phillip

From Me, to You…

From Me, to You...

Facing the demons of your past is one of the most difficult things for us to do as humans, especially when the things that have happened to us were out of our control at the time. I kept the secret of being molested to myself for a very long time. What I realize now, is that it set the stage for how I would deal with most, if not all, the problems I faced and how I communicated with people.

The fear of what my Uncle, mother or anybody else would do to retaliate is what kept me silent. I can remember playing different scenario's out in my mind. In one of them, I pictured going to my mother first. After I told her, she would burst into tears and begin to blame herself. I even imagined her hurting herself for not being there to protect me.

While that fear remained, as I got older, it was the idea of other people finding out what happened and the potential of them looking at me differently, which made me hide it even more. We read about child molestation cases almost daily in the news. In most cases the victim is a young female. Even when you hear of adults coming forward later in life, typically you won't hear of a male revealing how they were sexually abused at a young age, especially if it was by another male.

I have dealt with that over and over again. Because for us as men the question becomes, "will people question my masculinity?" "What other questions will I open myself up to?" I had to realize this horrible act was not a reflection on me or my sexuality. It had to do with him and his issues. I can speak about it without shame today because I am confident with myself. And that confidence came through faith in God and His forgiveness, forgiving myself, then forgiving my assailant. Through it all I have found, once you expose a spirit and confess that it dwells within you, God gives you the power to cast it from you. But you must first confess that it is there.

If you are someone who has been sexually abused in your past, I challenge you to talk about it. Once you express how you truly feel, you will be surprised how it will help to heal your pain. It will also

From Me, to You…

build your confidence in other areas of your life. The only requirement is that you must first deal with the anger. If you attempt to confront your past with an angry heart, the only closure you may directly or indirectly seek is vengeance. Forgiving others becomes much easier when you first forgive yourself.

If you or anyone you may know is dealing with abuse please call 1-800-799-7233. God Bless.

"You therefore, my son, be strong in the grace that is in Christ Jesus. And the things that you have heard from me among many witnesses, commit these to faithful men who will be able to teach others also. You therefore must endure hardship as a good soldier of Jesus Christ."
– 2 Timothy 2:1-3

Dear Pookie,

As I sit in front of this computer I find it difficult to carry any emotions. Not even resentment. I guess that's what happens over time. Time is supposed to heal all wounds. At least that's what they say. It has been such a long time since I have even allowed myself to think about you and our relationship (or lack there of). When I think back, I can hardly remember the times we spoke to each other, let alone times we spent together. Wait. I take that back. As I am writing this letter, a few memories do come to mind...

I vaguely remember one time when mom and I came to visit you. I couldn't have been more than four or five years old. I remember us walking down the street together one day and some lady telling Momma we all looked like brothers and sister. I don't know why I always smile about that. I guess because I can still picture the expression on Momma's face when the lady said it. Yeah, that's part of it. Being honest with myself, the biggest reason is, that's one of the happier memories I have of you and us.

From Me, to You…

Another one is the time I spent the weekend with you and your mother. I can still picture the house. She had a tan couch with flowers and a matching chair in the corner. You guys had an antique rotary telephone that sat on the end table, near the entrance to the dining room. Everything was covered in plastic. I even remember all of the pictures she had of you and Uncle Jermain plastered on the wall in the Dining Room. I had fun that weekend. I can't remember us doing anything specific but I do remember you letting me wear one of your Stetson hats. Man, I thought I was too cool (even back then). I guess that could be the reason why I like hats so much now. I never understood why you always wore them. As a matter of fact…why did you? You always wore suits too…why? I remember every time Momma would bring me to see you, or if I just ran into you at Uncle Jermain's Barber shop, you would always have on one of your suits and a sharp hat. You even had a suit on the time you came over Grandma's on your motor cycle. Momma was so mad at you when I burned my leg riding on the back. Suit or no suit, burn or no burn, those were good memories and I try to focus on them. But to be honest, it's hard to. My mind always goes back to the day you said you would come to my awards banquet when I played little league. You probably don't even remember…

When I was ten, I started playing PAL football for the Highland Park Hurricanes. When I first started I wasn't that good. But one day in practice we were doing a hitting drill called "Bull in the ring." Here is how it worked; the coaches would have us stand shoulder to shoulder and make a huge circle. That would make the ring. Then they would pick one person to be in the center and give him the football. The chosen one was the bull. The bull would run around the circle at least one full time and then on the next pass by he had to try and get out of the circle by running over one of the players who made up the ring. Before this day in particular, I use to be scared to death of this drill. I didn't even know how to tackle. As much as I hate to admit this, I didn't know how to do much of anything. Anyhow…a few people had gone through already and I managed to escape being chosen as the pathway out of the ring. At least until this one kid got the ball (I think his name was Devon). Even though Devon had a year of experience on me he was still a scrub. Some might even say as much of a scrub as I was at the time.

When Devon got the ball I just knew he was going to come at me. Why not? I was probably the skinniest kid on the team at the time. Everybody knew I couldn't bust a grape barefoot standing in a wooden bucket. So when he took the ball I knew I had to prepare myself. Although Devon may have been a scrub, he had me by at least three inches in height and ten pounds in weight. Devon ran around once. I could tell he was looking for a soft spot, someone specific, but who? Then he ran around a second time. On this pass buy, he looked me straight into my eyes. From the expression on his face and his sudden increase in speed around the circle, I could tell he had just found his weak link. I watched him as he turned the corner... faster and faster. My heart was racing. But as he turned the final corner and I realized the inevitable, I got a little pissed inside. *"This guy is trying to pick on me,"* I thought to myself. *"He knows he's bigger than me and I just started playing this year! Why won't he try one of the veteran guys like Jerry or Tone?"* The closer he got to me, the more upset I became. He just rounded the last turn. Here he comes! Charging at me, full speed, looking like George Forman going after the last piece of chicken from across the room. And before you knew it... WHACK!!!!!

Our helmets collided! I opened my eyes and he was flat on his back with my shoulder in his chest. I looked up from under my helmet and all the coaches and players were going NUTS!!!! *"That's it BLACK! THAT'S IT!!!!! THAT'S HOW YOU HIT!!!!!"* As I stood up I realized, I picked Devon up by both his legs like a cowboy would rope a steer, and slammed him into the ground. After everybody calmed down and I replayed everything in my mind; I remember saying to myself, "Oh... is that all I have to do?" From that day on the hog tie slam was my method for tackling. And I got really good at it. Before long I was starting at Linebacker. But you know all of this. I remember telling you over the phone.

We were talking almost every other day then. That made me happy because I felt like I was finally getting to know you. Through those conversations I realized where I got my voice from. It was amazing to me that you sang bass for a singing group with Uncle Jermain back in the day. And at the time I was singing bass for the group I was in too. I guess history does repeat itself.

We talked about a lot of stuff the night before the banquet. Momma had already told me she couldn't make it because of work. But I remember feeling as if she didn't want to come because she may have thought I wouldn't get anything. Who could blame her, after coming to my first three games and I didn't even get in. I got really good though, after I learned how to tackle, which is why I asked if you would come. I was so excited when you said yes, that I told all of my team mates. You told me you would meet me there, since you were catching the bus.

Only Auntie Diane had a car then and she was at work. So I had to walk to the banquet by myself. It wasn't too bad. I tried not to think about Momma or anyone else who couldn't make it. I knew they loved me just the same. So I just focused on my Daddy. I was smiling from ear to ear because I knew how sharp you would be dressed. I pictured you in an all white suit with your white Stetson brim on. All the way there I imagined my teammates coming up to me telling me how much I looked like you and how sweet your suit was.

When I got there most of the seats had been taken. And because of the walk I started to sweat a bit. I saw Anthony sitting with his mom and sister and there were a few empty seats in front of them. That was perfect, because those empty seats were facing the door. I didn't want to miss seeing you walk in. When I got to the table Ms. Crosley gave me a napkin to wipe my face. She told me how nice I looked. *"Thank you, but wait 'til you see my daddy."* "Is he coming?" She asked. *"Yeah, he will be here in a minute…"*

5:35pm came. 5:45pm… 5:46pm…, with every minute that passed like clockwork, I would look over my left shoulder toward the stage, then to the clock on the wall and back around to the door to see if you were there. Ms. Crosley must have caught on before I did because I remember her telling me you would be there. I concentrated on the door so much I forgot I was even at the ceremony. When they called my name up to accept the defensive player of the year award I almost missed it. Ms. Crosley had to tell me to go up. As I stood to walk toward the stage I almost tripped looking back at that door. I couldn't have imagined a more perfect moment than for you or Momma to come walking through that door just as I was accepting my trophy. But you didn't.

While I know they had been there the entire time, I couldn't help but notice all the other kids with at least one of their parents or family members. I sat for as long as I could, holding back the tears. I had a lump in my throat the size of a beach ball. *"Where are you going sweet heart?"* Ms. Crosley asked. *"Just to the restroom."* But I picked up my two trophies and walked out the door and went home.

Here I am sitting inside the library of Wayne State University, some twenty two years later, and I still can't help but cry when I think about it. *'I have to walk to the fuckin bathroom so these people in here studying don't look up and see me'*...

I would have felt better if you would have at least told me that you just couldn't make it. I was already a little disappointed that Momma didn't come, but I knew not to expect her. But you, I told everybody you were going to be there! I just knew in my heart you wouldn't do that to me! But you did! YOU DID DADDY! WHY? What did I do? WHY DIDN'T YOU EVER SHOW? NO BIRTHDAY CALLS! NO CHRISTMAS CARDS! NO FOOTBALL GAMES! NO NOTHING!!!!!!!!!!!!

But you know what?… After that, I stopped looking. I stopped wondering. I stopped asking. I stopped caring. But just like T and the boys from school, I wasn't going to let you stop me from being a better person. I dream of having a son of my own one day. I will love and play with him every day if God allows me to! There will not be a day that goes by that he won't know his Daddy loves him. I will read to him, tuck him in at night, and go to his games, plays or whatever else he decides to do. I could never understand why you didn't feel the same way about me.

One day while I was at my Grandmother's house I was watching Fresh Prince. In the episode Ben Vereen played the role of Will Smith's father. After years of not being around, they finally reunited and began to hang out again, and just when Will lets his guard down his dad disappointed him again by leaving without him. Will had just brought him a gift. It was a statue of a man holding his son in his lap. I never knew until the moment Will slammed that statue on the table and fell into his Uncle's arms just how much I did want you around. I did want to know. I realized how much I did care. As the tears leaped uncontrollably from my eyes I called the one person who I thought may be able to answer the same question Will posed to his Uncle on that show…

"Hello…"
I couldn't gather the words right away. I sat there with my eyes closed for a minute trying to fight through the pain in my throat. But nothing.

"Hello…"

"HELLO, IS ANYBODY THERE?"
Just before she almost hung up, with a cracking sob filled whisper, I managed to simply say…

"Momma…"
She quickly responded still unaware of how I was feeling, *"Hey baby…"*

Again I cried, *"Momma…"*

"Baby what's wrong!?"

I couldn't manage to hold it in any longer I screamed as loud as I could *"MOMMA!?… WHY-DON'T-HE-WANT-ME!?"*

Momma hung up the phone immediately. She her boyfriend Alvin drove to my Grandmothers fast as they could. I felt ashamed. By then I was already seventeen and a senior in high school. I was practically grown in my eyes. I shouldn't be crying like this. I shouldn't have allowed my emotions to take over the way that I did. Why did I feel so overwhelmed to the point of needing to talk to someone?

I had to realize later that I was human too. What I was feeling was real. Keeping it bottled up inside didn't help in anyway. For years I thought by not thinking about you and just moving on with my life; I was somehow dealing with the pain. Looking at the positive side of things only keeps a wound covered for so long. Eventually you have to remove the bandage for it to properly heal. The talk helped. If you can remember, I got your number from Uncle Jermain to call you again. It was the talk between Momma and I that made the difference. I can't even remember all she said. I only remember how good it felt to finally tell her I was hurting inside. How relieved I felt after crying while she and Alvin hugged me. I always wanted to talk to her and ask questions about the two of you. I was afraid she would be upset, feeling as if I didn't think she was enough. I didn't want her to think I didn't appreciate the things she did for me all on her own. So I kept my thoughts and questions bottled up inside.

The next day I went to Jermain's shop to get your number. We started communicating again from time to time. If you can remember, you even came to one of my high school games after that. It didn't matter to me that you only saw five minutes of the 4th quarter. You showed up. That was right around the time you started getting sick.

From Me, to You…

We lost contact for a while. Then my Grandmother called to say you and Jermain came by the house looking for me. It seemed like we kept playing phone tag. Or maybe that's how I want to remember it. To think, I didn't make an honest effort to even try to talk to you…it hurts now. If I had let go of the past and allowed us to start over again, on a clean slate, maybe things would have turned out different.

Which is why when Momma called me and said you were in the hospital again I knew I had to come see you. I can remember thinking about all the things I wanted to talk to you about and tell you, but I froze, and it was the same surface conversation we always had. It seemed like after you and I both answered the old question of "How you been?" We always reached for the rest of the conversation. I have to tell you though, I was really happy when you pulled out the clippings from when I made the news paper. I smiled so big on the inside after saying to myself "he does love me. He must have been keeping up with me all this time." Whether that was reality or not it wasn't relevant in my eyes. By the time I walked out I had a new since of hope for us as father and son. So when I got the phone call that morning from Momma I lost it for a while….

It was about 7:15am on a Friday. Even though I had a class at 8am I hadn't got out of bed yet. The sound of the phone ringing is what forced me up. For a minute I thought my roommate was going to pretend he didn't hear it. I would have been mad as hell if I had to jump down from the top bunk to answer and it was for him. After the third ring he rolled out of bed and grabbed it. I was thinking "Boy you just don't know what you did for yourself." He immediately sat the phone on the desk next to the computer. "It's for you." I climbed out of bed wondering who could it be at this time of the morning and what in the world could they want? We didn't have any assignments due so I knew it wasn't a classmate.

"Hello?…"

"Hey baby."

"Oh, hey Ma... what's going on?"

"Well baby..."

"Well what?"

"It happened."

"What do you mean?"

"He passed..."

I tried to be strong. I knew if I showed any emotion Momma would want to come to my rescue. I tried to delay my feelings by redirecting my focus to her.

"You ok Momma?"

"Oh I'm fine! Are you ok?" She replied, as if to say it had no effect on her at all. And as much as I tried to keep it together for her, she could hear the cracks in my voice toward the end. When we hung up the phone all I could do was go into the bathroom and breakdown. My roommate respectfully waited until I came out and gave me a hug. *"I'm sorry bro,"* he said with all sincerity.

I never got to ask you about how things were when you were my age. How you and Momma met. Where did you go when you were sad, happy or just wanted to get away? I never had a chance to ask you about girls. What to say, how to dress or how to act. Do I have any siblings? At that moment the missed birthday's, holidays, sports banquets, academic awards... the sporadic phone calls and broken promises... the no shows and where did you go's... the fact you were a pimp and dealt in the drug game... none of that mattered. One of the things that hurts the most now is the fact that I cannot remember for the life of me the last time I told you I love you. The last time you held me in your arms and said, "I love you… son." I would give anything to hear you say "I am proud of the man you have become. You did it Phillip… YOU-did it." That's all I wanted from you.

Now that I am older and have a better understanding of my purpose; I now realize that it was not you, nor momma who kept us apart. The Lord knew that while the pain would be deep, the purpose would be deeper. I know full well now more than ever that your absence allowed for His presence. Because even though you were not there (by choice or circumstances), He kept His hands on my life and provided someone to fill in for you in almost every area. And Dad, please don't take these words the wrong way. Those designated people are no longer meant to carry the pain that I felt. Rather they were meant to give you more insight to who I am, and who I had become. So I thank you. I thank you for anything you have ever done openly or even in secret. I thank you for the things you had the heart to do, and for the things that you may not have been destined to do. I forgive you for any wrongs that I previously held over your life and even in your death. I love you Daddy.

Little Phillip

From Me, to You…

Growing up without a father is difficult on many levels. No matter how many presents, hugs, kisses or events your mother attends; while you love her for it and appreciate what she has done, nothing replaces having "your father" there with you. There are so many questions we have throughout life. The answers, perspective and advice you receive from a woman will be naturally different than that of a man.

There is no secret we are living in a fatherless nation and time. Where our children are forced to raise themselves and learn things on their own understanding or just as TD Jakes put it in his book "HEMOTIONS", "through the wisdom of their peers." The blind are leading the blind and we are all falling into a ditch. In a time where the roles and definition of a man changes almost on a daily basis, depending on which direction the winds of society are blowing, it becomes incredibly difficult (if not impossible) to gain a sense of who you really are.

Pastor, author, and community activist Bishop TD Jakes, posed this simple question, in one of his DVD series titled "Into the Hearts of Men", *"What did your father name you?"* He further explained, *"…from the beginning of time it has always been the role of the father to name the male child. And whether you know it or not, your father did just that. No matter what role he did or did not play in your life, who he was and still is today has affected the way you view the world and deal with others. The question we must ask ourselves is, 'Am I comfortable with that identity'?"*

For years I identified myself as being a little ugly black boy, with no real friends, a dark secret, and a father who did not want him. Every day, I buried those thoughts in the soil of my soul and hid behind a mask. I walked around with a chip on my shoulder; quick tempered, waiting for an opportunity to show people how tough I was.

I wanted people to fear me so they would be too afraid to look beyond my surface and see that I was truly afraid.

Respect is what it is all about - at least for young black men. We are willing to do almost anything to protect our position and image of manhood. The problem is, the image that we have developed may be a hologram. Now more than ever, we need the men of this world to step up and stand strong in the community. We have too many children (and some adults) who are suffering because they have lacked the balance that comes from having a proper male perspective in their lives. The "figure it out along the way" approach to teaching is out dated and does not work. If you are a man reading this book, I challenge you to get involved in some way. Whether it is to join a mentoring program, coach a little league team, or simply start by communicating with the families on your block. Do something. We need it. Desperately.

Dear Antwone Fisher,

Your story touched me greatly when I had the opportunity to see your movie. I was obviously able to relate having been molested as a child and growing up without my father. I admired your persistence to find out where you came from. I can only imagine the joy you felt when you finally found your father's relatives.

While there were many elements of your life I read about in your book and scenes from the movie that pierced my heart; nothing impacted me more than this poem you wrote.

Who will cry for the little boy?

By Antwone Fischer

"Who will cry for the little boy, lost and all alone?

Who will cry for the little boy, abandoned without his own?

Who will cry for the little boy? He cried himself to sleep.

Who will cry for the little boy? He never had for keeps.

Who will cry for the little boy? He walked the burning sand.

Who will cry for the little boy? The boy inside the man.

Who will cry for the little boy? Who knows well hurt and pain.

Who will cry for the little boy? He died and died again.

Who will cry for the little boy? A good boy he tried to be.

Who will cry for the little boy, who cries inside of me?"

Even as I read it to myself today, I often have to fight back tears. I asked myself the same question of "Who" for years. I often wondered, *"Does anyone care about how I feel? Is there anyone who will stand up for me? Someone who cares enough about me to hear and feel my pain? When will I ever find a person I can trust enough to see me* cry and not judge me as being less than a man? Who will look past my smile and see my tears? Who?"

You inspired me to share my testimony and deal with my pain. Now I have found the answers that I have so desperately sought. Thank you.

Phillip Mozelle Black

From Me, to You…

"If they are talkin about you, that means you are doing something worth talkin about." **–Unknown**

Dear Aunt Jackie,

I love you so much. You have always taken care of me. Thank you for allowing me to stay with you all of those summers, as a child, so I could play with Joel and Charles. Even though we didn't have much, we always had fun.

We would have movie nights, popping Jiffy Pop over the stove. I loved the way the butter smelled as it melted over the steaming kernels. I especially liked when you put it the bowl and sprinkled a little seasoning salt and hot sauce on it, MAN! The only bad part about movie night was having to sit through a movie Big Lewis already saw. He would say each line before the actors, throughout the ENTIRE movie. But that didn't spoil our time together.

Even though we had government food from Focus Hope for the most part, we ate happily and often. The only thing I wished for us kids, was to not have had pork and beans and hot dogs, or smoked sausage with corn and rice so often during the week. It seemed like that was the main rotation. Too funny! Like I said, we may not have had much, but you always took care of us.

I even remember how you would sometimes hand wash our clothes in the bathtub, then dry them on the door of the stove when we couldn't afford to go to the laundry. The way you put your love and strength into those hands, no one could ever tell the difference. I love you so much for that and so many other things. I am not sure if I ever shared this with you Auntie. But did you know I give you the credit for breaking me out of my complex about being dark? Well I do. I know you don't remember this so I'll tell you the story....

It was a normal Friday morning in early March. We were at the end of one of the coldest winters I had ever felt. It seemed as if there was a blizzard once a week. Remember that? It was the winter of '86-'87. I was getting ready for school (and you know Momma didn't play when it came to getting to that bus on time). So I quickly finished my oat meal, and ran to the bus stop. You know I didn't mind catching the bus alone; by the time we moved on Fairfield I was a veteran to public transportation. I even knew how to take a transfer. On my normal route I would get off at Rosa Parks and walk about five blocks to the school. Along the way I would see at least one of my friends, usually Latonya or Armon. Everyone else would meet, either on the playground, or in the hall just before the bell rang. And that's where it normally began...

"DAMN! Yo' hair nappy as hell!"... "Didn't you have that on yesterday?" Or, "I saw yo' mamma last night...." And just like that, the "capping" began. "Man, you so ugly... you have to bathe in sausage grease to get yo' dog to play with you." After that a quiet outburst of laughs would ring out and it was on, and some embarrassed kid would reply, "Oh yeah? You so short you model for trophies!" "Shhhhhhhh..." Dr. Essel, our principle, would say as everybody tried to hold it in.

Capping was a fun game to stand on the sidelines and observe. And now that I am older and more comfortable with being me, it's a pretty fun game to play too, but back then, you know I didn't have any fun. Not only was I self-conscious but I was also not very quick witted. As a matter of fact, I did my best not to hurt anyone's feelings; thinking my kindness would make others want to treat me the same way. Well in adulthood and childhood alike, most people tend to take kindness for weakness, and when it came to a tenacious game like "capping" there was no room for sensitivity and emotions. Weakness is often sniffed out and preyed upon; especially if you are found laughing on the sidelines. Usually you are drafted into the game by the person who is losing.

"*What-choo laughin' at blackie?*" And with that simple question, the attention and tables have turned away from the seemingly loser to the one everyone knows, can't take the heat. "*This nigga got the nerve to be named Black!*" The laughs begin to seem louder... "*You so black you put finger prints on charcoal!*" My smile quickly drops, hoping it will make him stop. "*When Mrs. Stevens calls yo name, I be like... you aint lying!*" I unzip my coat to catch a breeze. "*And you sweatin! This nigga so black he sweat WD40!*" And just as the lump in my throat begins to form... "*rrrrrrrrrRRRing!*" "*Okay students; walk slowly and to the right of the hall.*" Saved by the bell again. Often times I would make a stop in the boys room to gather myself. "*I can't let them see me cry.*" Nothing could have been worse in my mind than to not only be dark and ugly; but to top it off, I would be known as a punk. The laughter would continue slightly up the stairs but usually by the time we got to the classroom it seemed as if everyone had moved to something else. During class everything was fine.

I transferred to Liberty from Midland the year before in the fourth grade. Although, it took a little while for people to get use to me, I managed to make a few friends. You know how being the new kid can be? I remember trying to do everything to get people to like me, especially Lisa. I tried to impress her once by bringing her an envelope full of costume jewelry. Two problems with that, she didn't like jewelry and I got it from my grandmother's jewelry box. When Lisa took the envelope up to Mrs. McCarther's desk I thought I would die. That is one whoopin' I will NEVER forget.

I even pretended I knew how to tap dance once during show and tell, but no one told me dress shoes were not tap shoes. Over and over again I tried to gain acceptance. Once people found out I could draw, they seemed to begin to like me, at least most of the time. However, a lot of the friends I made through my art or by whatever means in my fourth grade class were not with me in the fifth. So I had to try all over again.

"*rrrrrrrRRRRRing!*" "*Ok children it is lunch time. Put your books away and grab your coats in case you go outside.*" I liked going outside the last fifteen minutes for lunch. We usually got at least one game of basketball in. I couldn't shoot very well so I hardly made captain. But Anthony or Jason would pick me because I hustled and played defense. On those days everything seemed great, especially if they got into an argument about who would pick me for their team. I felt like one of them. When the weather was bad or when the kids were too loud during the lunch period we would have to stay inside. You can imagine what the guys did to past the time. "*Look at Phil... damn he black.*" Then it seemed as if everyone in the lunch room would turn directly at me. "*Dude... what I don't understand is... why would yo Momma name you Black?...why would she do that to you?*" More laughs were added to the orchestra. "*I mean you are BLACK as Hell!*" And again, without anything witty to say in return, I sat in silence. Internally saying the same things to myself or even asking the very same question... "*Why did my name have to be Black?*" It would always be tough to handle the on slot of insults while they were coming, yet I usually managed to block them out of my mind after an hour or so. By the time school let out and I got home or to Gran'moan's, I would be ok. However, that day hurt a little more than usual.

Since it was the weekend, instead of catching the bus home I walked to Gran'moan's. (By the way, you are going to have to tell me again, who actually started calling Grandma that). I would stay there most weekends and my Mom would come to pick me up on Sundays. I loved to stay over Gran'moan's. You brought Joel a Nintendo just like mine so we could have something to play there too. We would play Legend of Zelda all night long. It's funny now as I look back on how you all raised us; we were more like brothers than cousins. Whenever you, Momma, Aunt Diane or even Gran'moan saw a nice outfit and had some extra money; you would buy it in two different colors, one for Joel and one for me. Aside from playing with Joel, the best part about being there on the weekends was the good eating.

Don't get me wrong, Momma can cook. But Gran'moan could throw what some people call, *DOWN!* Gran'moan could take twenty dollars worth of food stamps and make a meal fit for a king and have enough to feed a football team. I always felt better after a hug and kiss from Gran'moan. Her home made fried chicken helped too. After a long weekend of video games, "pick-um-up mess-um up" and good eating I was ready to get back home.

I wouldn't see Momma until it was time to go home on Sunday, usually around four or five in the evening but this particular day, I called Momma a little earlier, and told her I was upset. She came over early on Saturday to pick me up. "*What's wrong baby?*" She asked with a sincere tone of concern that only mothers have, and before I could even think about what to say, I burst out crying, "*THEY KEEP TALKIN-BOUT ME!*" I screamed as tears spilled from my eyes like an over flowing sink.

"*Aw..., baby it's gone be o-kaaaay... what happen?*" Momma asked.

"*They keep calling me black... and UGLY!*"

"*Awww...,*" as she hugged me and wiped away the tears. "*Baby you are not ugly. All they can say is that you are dark. Mommy dresses you nice, keeps your hair cut and you are beautiful baby.*" Despite her genuine attempt to make me see her reality and what she thought of me, I could only focus on the picture imbedded in my mind. The tears continued to flow and the sobs got longer. I couldn't hear her words of encouragement because I was focused on the same question that seemed to follow me for most of my life. "*Why me?*"

I wouldn't intentionally hurt anyone. "*Why me?*" I just want to be their friend. "*Why me?*" And every time I asked myself that seemingly unanswerable question... the blade from the jokes would cut deeper and deeper as I replayed them in my mind. But Momma knew how to make it all better.

That Saturday night Momma came to pick me up after work. We rode around for about an hour talking. We even stopped for my favorite ice cream, vanilla cone with a cherry hard shell dip. We talked and talked, and talked and talked for what seemed like forever.

Finally we went back home. I went directly to my room to get settled, but momma called me into her room. *"Here Man, try these on."* Momma had gone out during work and brought me three new outfits. I smiled from ear to ear. *"Ooooh, thank you Momma!"* I always liked clothes. While I rarely asked my mother for anything specific she always seemed to know what the latest fashions were.

Momma bought me a pair of denim jeans with a collar shirt to match, a pair of khaki color corduroys with a matching sweater and lastly a pair of white jeans and a white sweat shirt. I tried on all three and of course I loved each and every one. But I am sure you can guess which one I loved the most. You got it, the all white outfit. *"Let Momma see... Oooh look at my baby...So handsome."* Momma always said things like that especially when I didn't feel so hot. She told me once recently how she never understood why I couldn't see it.

After I finished trying on the clothes I took my bath. Before I went to bed Momma called me into her room one last time. *"Sit down."* We both sat side by side at the foot of her bed.

"Look at me. You know I love you right?"

"Mmmhmmm," I murmured.

"I know I'm your mother and you think we are suppose to say things like this, but baby you are beautiful. The only reason they say the things they do is because they are jealous. You are not ugly. When you get older, you will find out that most women prefer a dark skinned man. Watch what I tell you."

"Mmmmmhmmm," I murmured again thinking *"I can't wait to get older then."*

That night, I lay in bed staring at the sealing, reviewing all the jokes as I rewound the video of my mind. I even went back to the time I was playing basketball on Louise, just around the corner from

Gran'moan. There was a house we use to play at across the street from my friend Clyde's home. Even though there weren't any kids our age that lived there, the older guy that did would always let us shoot hoops in his backyard. I liked going there because his sister, who may have been four or five years older than us would come outside sometimes and talk on the phone. SHE WAS BEAUTIFUL! One day she came out back while we were playing. Of course the game got more intense the moment she stepped onto the back porch.

"Foul!? Damn you a hack!" Clyde would scream out just loud enough for Shannon to hear.

"Quit cryin!" I would say so that I looked just as tough.

As the game continued, and Shannon went in and out of the house, we grew a little thirsty. Clyde knew the family pretty well since he lived right across the street. So when we took a break he asked Shannon to get us some water; which she did without hesitation. As we were sitting on the porch out of nowhere Clyde says,

"Shannon I know somebody that likes you."

Immediately I caught a legion of butterflies in my stomach and my heart fell to the floor.

"WHO!?" She asked forcefully, yet curiously.

"I can't tell you his name," Clyde said with a devilish grin.

"Well what does he look like?" Shannon asked as her curiosity increased.

"All I can say is, he's dark." Clyde replied.

To this day, I don't know if she knew that it was me Clyde was referring to or not. But when she heard that it seemed as if her eyes and entire focus shifted toward me to deliver her response just in case it was.

"Uuuuhhh! I HATE dark skin boys! They are SO UGLY! My daddy black and I HATE BLACK MEN! Whoever it is tell him NO!"

When you hear comments like that most of your life from the people you interact with, no matter how special, beautiful or talented your mother thinks you are; it just doesn't take away the pain. I cried for nearly an hour that night until I fell asleep.

The next morning Momma cooked breakfast before she went to work. Even though I was nine I was ok with staying home alone. If I got scared I would just turn on all the lights in the house. After Momma left I must have tried on each of my new outfits twenty times separately. I was excited. I could not wait to show off my new gear.

"They won't talk about me tomorrow," is all I could think.

When Momma got home from work she asked if I had everything ready for school. I figured she had to go to her second job at the Gas station in the morning, so she wanted to be certain.

"Make sure you don't forget anything because I'll be gone to work before you get up."
"Yes ma'm."

Before I turned to walk in my room she said, *"Baby I know you like that white outfit but don't wear that one just yet."*

"Yes ma'm," I said as my heart stopped. How did she know that was the one I wanted to put on? But the next day take a wild guess as to what I wore? That's right.

That morning I was about twenty minutes early to the bus stop. Hair perfectly brushed, outfit and shoes gleaming. I even put Vaseline on my face and I HATED when Momma would do that. She said it was to keep me from being ashy and protect my face from the cold. But that wasn't how the kids at school saw it. But none of that mattered. Today was going to be different. All the girls, especially Lisa, were going to go crazy over my new pearl white outfit. And the guys... All of those fellahs that normally talked about me were going to come over and shower me with compliments, asking where did I get that "sweet" outfit from? I had it all scripted in my mind. It was a full proof plan. That is until the dialogue in my mind collided with the reality of the day...

From the moment I walked into that dreaded hallway, my morning joy and excitement was transformed to humiliation.

"DAMN! Hold on nigga… hold on… now I was just jokin' before. I thought you was kiiiiiiind-of black. But seeing you in all white? Dude it aint no doubt… YOU BLACK AS FUCK!"

All eyes turned toward me in laughter. Boys and girls!

"Dog do you see this nigga?"

I unzipped my coat because the temperature was rising faster than normal. I needed some air…I couldn't break down

"Aye yall… Crayola got a new color. It's called Phil BLACK!"

'My heart starts pounding. I began to get dizzy. The lump in my throat is growing at the speed of a heat seeking missile. Tears are forming in my eyes like valley in the midst of a flood. The only option I am left with is to break the golden rule of capping… walk away.'

I started doing the 'pee pee' dance to play it off. Then I began to slowly drift away as they were still throwing gut punches to my self-esteem and ego. But when I got around the corner I darted to the bathroom like an Olympic sprinter. I couldn't even make it into the door path before the tears started pouring out. I felt like such a fool. *"Momma told me not to put this dumb outfit on! She told me! I'm so stupid! Hard headed! They don't like you! They never did like you! They won't like you!"* Over and over again I shouted these words to myself in my mind as I hid in the stall.

Finally the bell sounded. I waited until I thought everyone had cleared the hall before I went to class; hoping they had forgotten and everything would go back to normal as usual. But the moment I got in the room it seemed as if EVERYONE in the class had already heard about the outfit and how I ran off like a little girl.

As I walked to the coat room without making direct eye contact with anyone, I could see the guys all smirking in my peripheral. As I proceeded past the chalkboard I felt like a duck at the carnival getting shot by every grin and snicker. Suddenly, I thought to myself, I better keep my coat on. At least they won't see the outfit that way. But that turned out to be yet another dumb move considering how easily I sweat.

Feeling the pressure of what seemed to be the entire class staring at me, and the heat generated from this coat, it only took about forty five SECONDS before the sweat began to rain down my face. It was so bad that Mrs. Stevens even noticed from across the room.

"*Phillip, hang your coat up son,*" she said with concern.

But the only thing I noticed was that if everyone hadn't been looking at me at this point, they were now.

"*I'm fine.*" Why did I say that? It was like we were in the hall all over again.

"*Quiet down*", Mrs. Stevens commanded. "*Go hang your coat up. You cannot wear it during class.*"

So I walked slowly to the room hoping the long, short walk would give me enough time to cool down. But by then the damage had already been done. Not only was I in a gleaming white outfit, but now I am sweaty too. I stayed in the coat room hoping the sweat would dry up within a matter of seconds. It was pretty cool in there. But after no more than sixty seconds Mrs. Stevens came to the door.

"*Come on out and take your seat.*"

More snickers… smirks, laughs, private jokes. "What had I gotten myself into?"

"*Quiet! Pull out your homework, get your notebooks and begin your bell work,*" Mrs. Stevens said.

And though the room reached complete silence, and physically I couldn't hear anything else, in my mind it was still going on.

After a couple of hours, things had pretty much settled; within myself I mean. We were well into the lesson for the day and I was no longer dripping with sweat. And then it happened.

"Ok children, I need to speak with Mr. Green. Continue to work and I will be right back. Mrs. Donalds is going to be listening, so behave."

Mrs. Stevens couldn't have made it out of the room a full ten steps before I heard, *"Pssst… sweaty? Hey! Sweaty McNasty!?"* The room erupted instantly with laughter. *"Shhhhhhh!"* Someone said in the middle of their own laugh.

"Man, I feel bad for you. You black, ugly and sweaty!" That was the last thing I remember hearing.

All of a sudden I became temporarily deaf. I closed my eyes to visualize myself in another place, in another time, in another body. It was so much happier in my mind. There, I was cool. I was handsome. I wore the best clothes. I had the best smile. All the girls liked me and all the boys wanted to be my friend. I loved it there. I wanted to be there, anywhere but here.

When I opened my eyes I realized that only a few seconds had passed. The kids were still talking, laughing and joking. Mrs. Stevens had not yet returned and Mrs. Donalds did not come in to save me. The only thing I didn't notice right away was that a single tear had managed to escape down my cheek. When I finally recognized it was there; and that my apparent crying was the new reason for the laughter, my body went num. I stood up from my desk and walked to the coat room.

"Phil!… Phil!… " the main jokester pleaded.

I got my coat and gathered my things. All the while, I recall people were talking to me. But it was like passing by a picture window watching someone eat and you want to get their attention but because of the glass between the two of you, they just can't hear you. Therefore they ignore you.

"Phil!… Phil! (while he is still laughing)… *ok man. I'm sorry. Sit down man."* As I passed by him. *"PHIL!"* He whispers with force as I walk out the door.

I don't know if any teachers or adults noticed me. Nor did I even care. I walked from school in the middle of the day back home alone. The entire time all I could think about as the tears fell was *"Why?"*

I knew my mother would still be at work. So I wasn't afraid she would find me. When I got home, I walked upstairs, took off my coat and laid my book bag on the bed. I knew why I was there. I went directly to my mother's room. Opened her night stand drawer and grabbed her twenty two caliber pistol and went to the bathroom. Shaking with anger, hurt and hatred toward myself I stood in the mirror for over a half hour crying with that gun to my head. *"Why? Why don't they like me? Why am I so ugly? No one would miss me."*

What kept me from pulling that trigger was imagining my mother coming home and seeing me laid out on the floor - how could I do that to her. If nobody else, my Momma loved me. She liked me. She thought I was handsome. She thought the world of me. And it was that day, that exact moment I said to myself...

"If I am ugly... if I am too black... I am going to make sure my body looks sweet, and that I have a dollar for ever tear I have cried, and I am going to make sure everyone that I meet throughout my life knows that they matter and someone loves them."

It was still pretty tough after that. Until one day I came to Gran'moan's after school and you saw me sitting at the dining room table crying. You came and sat down with me and asked what was wrong?

"They keep talkin about be at school."

"What do they say to you?"

"They call me black and ugly."

Then you asked, *"Well, who's talkin about you?"*

"Anthony, Michael, Armon..."

I will never forget your next question for as long as I live. It was so simple but yet affective and right on time. *"Those are all boys, why do you care about what boys think?"*

From Me, to You...

With that, my tears stopped like someone shut off a faucet. I never looked at it that way before. All I could say then was, *"You're right."*

Thank you so much Auntie, you did more than you know. Love you.

Phillip

by Phil Black

From Me, to You…

My Aunt was able to shift my thinking in a direction I did not know existed. That simple question allowed for me not only to see who talked about me but why. In addition, once I recognized the source of all the ridicule it allowed me to listen out for the compliments.

I remember once getting my hair cut sometime after that, at the barber shop on McNichol's and Third. The shop was full that morning with men and women. The barber my mother normally had to cut my hair was not there so a lady cut it instead. After I was done, I paid her and walked out. While leaving the shop I heard one of the ladies in the chair sitting near the barber say…

"He is so cute. I know he got him a little girl friend."

I began to hear compliments like that more often. Who knows, good things may have always been said about me. I had turned a deaf ear to any positive words because all I focused on was the negative. More and more I began to be comfortable with my skin. Especially when I learned the power of beating people to the punch.

I saw an episode of Full House once. In it, one of the girls had been dealing with something similar. Someone advised her to tell the jokes before the other kids did. By doing so she would take away their verbal ammunition and the sting of their insults. I took that advice and it worked. I started saying things like, *"It's a Black thing… you wouldn't understand."* The more jokes I told about myself, the more other people laughed. As a result they were less likely to talk about me for their own entertainment. Overtime I gained more comfort because I did not take myself so seriously.

I have come to realize that everyone has at least one thing about themselves they would change or one noticeable flaw that makes them uncomfortable. Yet it tends to be that one thing that makes them unique. I think we would see less plastic or cosmetic surgery if we learned how to except and celebrate one another's differences. I have grown to love being in my skin. I could not see myself any other way.

From Me, to You…

"It is only hard to quit something one time. After that it gets easier and easier. Before you know it, that's all you have become."
–Coach Keith Bradford

Dear Coach Runn,

I know it has been a while since I came to the High School to see you. How have you been? Things are going well with me in general, finally working on my dream of entering into the public speaking arena. Don't think I am abandoning my art work. I will begin to draw even more, now that I am laid off. I'll also get the chance to come back and visit the students too. The last time I was there you spoke to me about a desperate need for alumni to come back from time to time. These kids really need to see more live examples of maturity that came from where they come from. Most importantly they need to see how someone who is older but closer in age conducts themselves and communicates with people. Things are so different from when I was in school there… we both agreed.

When my peers and I were coming through school, our era still had respect for adults and authority. To say "I am going to call home" actually meant something. There was a fear of consequences for our actions. Today it seems as if everyone is so desensitized and detached from reality, the basic values for human life no longer exist. But this is no secret and it is nothing new. I guess I just simply wanted to say thank you for all that you have given me. I appreciate the lessons I learned from you, Coach Dean, Twin, Marvin, Coach Jackson and Pep. I remember I didn't always feel that way. As a matter fact I didn't really like you when I first got to high school. But overtime I understood why you did the things you did, said the things you said and carried yourself in the manner in which did. It was your example of a man that also made me want to be a Que.

It was the summer of '88. Joel was getting ready to go to Highland Park High himself. He was getting older and beginning to make a lot of new friends and I was still dealing with the issues of elementary school. One new friend he made was Jamil. Jamil had little brother named Curtis. Jamil and Curtis had a really nice house. The first time I saw it from the outside, it looked like a small castle, white with brown trim. Perfectly sculpted shrubbery (it wouldn't give it justice to call them bushes). When we walked in I thought I was on Lifestyles of the Rich and Famous. They had everything. Between Jamil and Curtis they must have had at least 2000 pairs of shoes. Okay, maybe not 2000, but way more than I had ever seen.

I always liked to play over there. At least until Curtis started acting spoiled. It seemed like the only game he ever wanted to play was Altered Beasts. I liked the game too, but after we beat it, the thrill was gone. Joel and I visited frequently, but it wasn't until after I saw an old step show called "Stomp" that I paid attention to all the plaques going up the staircase of their house.

"What are these for?" I asked.

"My dad is a Kappa. I think he was like their Grand Pole something…" Jamil replied.

"What is that?"

"Just a fancy way for saying president."

When I saw the colors and the pictures I immediately remembered the guys throwing the canes.

"I saw them doing some step on TV. It was kind of sweet. So they are called Kappa?"

"Yeah, he wants me to be one but I'm not sure." Jamil seemed to know a lot about them so it made me ask, *"Who are the guys that wear gold boots?"*

"THOSE ARE THE QUES!" He said.

"Those dudes are rough man."

"I know, I saw them too. Those boots are BAD!"

Jamil and I talked about fraternities almost the entire time I was over there that day. It wasn't until I actually got to High School that I met a fraternity brother in person.

When I got to Highland Park High in the fall of 1991 it seemed as if I already knew half the people in the school. My cousin Angie was the first to attend. She didn't make a lot of friends there. I guess she really wanted to stay at Mumford. By the time I got there, Angie had graduated and Joel was now in his senior year. I imagine he was just as excited about me coming to school there as I was about going. Joel told everyone he knew that his little cousin was going to be a freshman that year. Throughout my time in high school my life was impacted by a lot of people. But you were one of the few to leave a lasting impression…

When we met, you were coaching the junior varsity basketball and football teams, and when I say you GOT ON MY NERVES! MAN! It seemed like I couldn't pick my nose without having to run laps. When I got to school in the fall I knew I was going to play football. At the time my mother was very protective of me because of my asthma.

One day after an intense practice I could not seem to catch my breath. I started wheezing pretty heavily. Mom rushed me the hospital because of an asthma attack that could not be subdued due to my broken inhaler. That night she said the three most hurtful words ever, "No more football." I was crushed. Football had become my outlet. I finally found something else I was actually good at, that drew people to me in a good way.

"Why Momma?" I asked barely able to utter the words for the sake of breathing.

"Baby, listen at you. You can hardly breathe. I don't want anything to happen to you."

I don't know about you. But the first thing that popped in my head was, *"What Momma don't know won't hurt her."*

After I got my doctor's note to return to school I went right back to practice. I don't know if you remember, but after you found out I had an asthma attack you eased up on me a little physically; but mentally and verbally, you turned it up.

"Man, I hate coach Runn. He always talking' shit! I mean DAMN! I get in the front of every line for drills. I run just as hard if not harder than everybody but he won't leave me alone!" I said complaining to Alvin, one of my teammates.

But before he could reply all I heard from around the corner was, *"SO WHAT!? So what I get in yo' ass... What are you gone do about it!?"*

"Nothing... all I can do is take it. I aint quittin'."

"That's right! You gone shut up and take it!" Then you said one of the first of many phrases to help shape my mentality.

"Remember this, if I get in yo' ass that means I see something in you. But if I ever STOP talking to you... then you need to worry. Because that means I've given up on you." I have used that as a philosophy for dealing with not only kids but people in general.

As you turned to walk away, my head bowed in embarrassment. My eyes glanced over the leather bag you always carried with you. I have always recognized it but have never paid any attention to the bag itself. Within a matter of seconds I noticed the bag was a deep purple rather than black or brown. *"Strange"* I thought. Then as you turned away from me I saw a gold emblem on the front of it. *"That's a Que bag!"* I thought to myself excitedly. After practice the next day I approached you in the locker room.

"Coach, that's a Que bag aint it?"

"You damn right! Why? You want to be a Que?" He replied with that 'yeah right' look on his face.

Yeah, I'm gonna be one when I get to college." I said with confidence.

"Well I tell you what, to get this (pointing down directly at the Omega shield on the front of the bag), *you have to have this."* You looked me dead in the eye and pointed towards your heart.

I don't know if it was the look in your eye or the conviction in your voice, but something moved inside me. I remember thinking to myself, *"Those dudes must be hard."*

If you recall, from time to time I would ask you questions about the fraternity and what I had to do to join. But whenever I asked about the process you would only say *"It aint for everybody."* I wasn't sure if you said it to scare me, but all it did was heighten my curiosity. Every now and again I would mess with you by making the Que sign or "Throwing up the Hooks" as we call it. And without fail you would always say,

"Don't make me whoop yo' ass!"… That was my laugh for the day.

When I realized you actually liked me and only wanted to see me get better, it felt good when you would talk about me. Or in this case, talk about beating me up. But one of my best memories came my senior year…

It was our second game of the season against River Rouge High. We had just come off a close win against U of D, where I scored the only touchdown of the game off a fumble recovery. It was the second half, no one was on the board yet but our defense had been playing soft at best. After a good halftime tongue lashing from Coach Twin, I made up my mind to do something about it. I finished the game with twelve tackles, a forced fumble and two touchdowns. One of which I scored by picking up a short punt (against the direction of coach Marvin) and ran it in. But the play which brought me the most joy came on a third down.

Rouge High was set in their normal Full House backfield. It was third down, with five yards to go for a first; we were initially thinking pass. But at the snap of the ball the flow of the play came in my direction. It was an option. After taking a false step back to cover the pass I quickly changed direction to take out the pitch man, or the Quarterbacks second option to give the ball to. As I crossed the line I gave a jab step toward the quarterback to make him think I was coming for him. But in a matter of seconds, after he took the bait he pitched the ball to my man. Still in position to make the tackle I hit the man with one shoulder and knocked the ball loose. Without any wasted motion I scooped the ball up and ran it in for a touchdown. The few fans, especially my Mom went bananas! Everyone ran to either, hit me on the helmet, slap my behind, punch me in the arm, throw a high five, or just give me a hug. It was almost the best feeling of that day. But it wasn't until you called out to me from the sideline as we set up for the kickoff that I felt as if I was on top of the world. You called out from the other side of the field and said...

"Throw it up!"

Thank you Coach for all that you've given me and more.

Black

Suburban Athletic

Highland Park 22, River Rouge 0.
Senior strong safety Phillip Black
sparked the Polar Bears (4-0, 2-0) by
scoring on a 25-yard punt return and a
25-yard fumble return. He also had 11
tackles. Senior tailback Andre Crosby
(11 carries, 100 yards) also scored, on a
55-yard run. Senior defensive end Law-
rence Haynes had seven solo tackles
and four assists. The Panthers are 1-3,
1-2.

by Phil Black

From Me, to You...

I was blessed to be mentored by coaches who truly cared about developing not only a young man's athletic abilities, but more importantly his character. My high school defensive back coach Dean or "Daddy D" as we called him, once told one of the best players on our team he couldn't play because of his grades. In fact, the way Daddy D put it was, *"Son your grades are so bad you couldn't play marbles for me."* Coach Dean didn't make any phone calls or extra concession for his players, he just simply sat them down until they got themselves together. Coach Dean wasn't the only one who set those types of standards.

My High School Basketball coach, Darnel Pepper also known as Coach Pep was known for putting kids in their place no matter how gifted they were. I remember once, a kid did a finger roll in practice rather than laying the ball off the glass, *"You'd better be damn lucky that crap went in, cause if you had missed it your ass would have been sittin' with me!"* He had standards and everyone knew it. My first day trying out for him I really wanted to leave an impression, so I made sure I stayed in front of the line during drills. When Pep finally walked in the gym we were running laps. I was leading everyone just as I planned. As I circled the floor past Coach Pep I got excited because I saw him looking at me from my peripheral. The next thing I heard behind me was, *"You!... You!"* I looked over my shoulder toward him, *"Yes... YOU!!... GET THE HELL OUT OF MY GYM!"* I was dumb founded. I stopped running and stood there with my heart racing wondering what the hell happened. "GET THE HELL OUT!" Shamefully I turned around and started walking toward the locker room. Coach Pep stopped me just before I hit the door. *"Come here son... do you want to play on this ball team?"* "Yes coach." *"Then take that damn ear ring out your ear, and don't ever wear it in my gym again!"*

While I hated to be embarrassed that way, I took it on the chin just as I did many times before and after. The standards by which those men lived taught me another level of respect for my elders and for myself. One may say "It is my choice to wear what I wish. Style my hair how I choose or even wear ear rings and tattoos." I agree. It is your personal choice. However when you are looking to play ball on another man or woman's court, you have to play by their rules.

I thank Coach Runn for challenging me to achieve the things that I desired. I appreciate my Coaches for seeing enough in me to "get and stay on my ass." They taught me to see myself better than what I was, and never to be satisfied with what I achieved. Today we pacify our youth by giving them everything they desire without teaching them the value of sweating for it. We bite our tongues fearing the loss of their friendship, rather than speaking the truth, to maintain our position as the elder. We use to have a saying in our organization, *"You don't even get an opinion until you have at least four years of service in."* The parents we grew up with did not care about being your friend. And while we hated to hear the words, *"Because I said so"*; we respected their position and knew not to question it. I am not saying we need to totally disregard our children's feelings and stop listening to what they have to say. What I am saying is, there has to be more of a balance with a higher percentage placed on being more of a mentor or parent than a partner.

"The only way to be heard is by speaking." –Kenneth Black

Dear Uncle Richard,

I did it man. I remember when I came to your place in Grand Rapids. You were really excited about the idea of me writing a book. I know at the time it may have seemed as if I was blowing the idea off or wasn't really listening. Obviously I was listening, but I was thrown back by your enthusiasm. All the wonderful things you said about me and how I impacted your life surprised me. You made mention of what you saw as being the turning point. I don't know if I went into detail then, when I agreed with you about that day. You were right, that was a turning point for me. I'll tell you why, if I have never told you the story…

You know how we use to always wear each other's clothes when I got to the eighth grade? Hard to believe I grew like that. I remember everybody (including me) thought I would be like six foot three or four. (Man did I get the short end). I use to get mad when you would sometimes take my clothes without asking but you always wanted me to ask you for yours. I'll never forget the time you yelled at me for wearing your Phillies jersey one afternoon. Then later that day I saw you with one of the shirts Momma had just brought for me. Times like those really made me feel like my opinion didn't matter. Especially considering no one would ever say anything to you about it.

From Me, to You…

I never felt as small and insignificant as I did when I came home from football one day; I brought a few snacks on the way home from school to have after I got out of practice. I ate the candy bar on the way but I left my chips on the kitchen table. When I came home I went straight to the kitchen. But my chips were no longer where I left them. So I looked on top and inside the fridge. I looked on the butcher block, on the kitchen counter, in all the cabinets and nothing. So with anger and frustration I started calling out, "Who took my chips?" Now you were only sitting a few feet away in the den reading the Sports section of the paper. Something already told me in my gut what happened, but out of fear I never came in to ask you directly. I walked to the bottom of the stairs and asked Gran'moan if she saw them.

"Yeah baby, they were on the table where you left them."

I got a little more upset. So I went out on the porch to yell out in the yard where Charles was playing,

"CHARLES! DID YOU EAT MY CHIPS!?"

He replied, *"Nooooo."*

At this point I was furious. But I also wanted to cry. I couldn't help but feel like I was just some insignificant nothing that any and everybody picked on. By then I knew what happened. But again, because I was too fearful of how you would react I took the passive aggressive approach. I came back in the house and just stood in the hall by the steps so Gran'moan could hear me again. I think you may have picked up on that yourself, which may have been the reason why you took the tone you did. Because not a second after I yelled those words again,

"Who ATE MY CHIPS!?"…

by Phil Black

I heard you say, *"I DID!!!!"*

No apologies… no I'll buy you another bag… You didn't say not a single word after. As a matter of fact you never even left your seat in the den. And the way you said it was with an undertone that suggested "Now what?"

All I could do was go upstairs and cry. Not because you ate the chips; not because you yelled and told me as if you didn't care. I cried that day because I couldn't help but feel as if nobody ever cared about how I felt. Nobody ever considered my feelings. They just took from me and talked about me. Nobody ever listened to me. So from that day on I remember thinking if he is going to take from me, I'm going to take from him. Which is how we got to the day I took your favorite Sun glasses.

I knew you were looking for them for weeks, and it actually only took days for my anger towards you to blow over, but by that time, I felt like it was too late to change my story. You understand…right? If I had given them back, saying that I found them, you would have never let me borrow them, and I would have had to steal them all over again. So I decided to keep them. But the day you came home early from playing basketball and saw me wearing them while I was walking down the street is one I will never forget.

I didn't realize you were in the passenger seat until you got about ten feet in front of me. As you drove by I could see your entire expression change. I knew it was over. My heart started pounding, my stomach fell to my feet and sweat started pouring down my face. And as much as I didn't want to, I turned around and walked back across the street to the house. I knew I had to give them back to you then. But what in the HELL kind of story could I have made up in less than sixty seconds? None! By the time we met at the steps of the porch you were FLAMING MAD.

Unc I don't know what part of that day you felt like made the difference to turn my attitude around. But it wasn't the fact I thought you were going to kill me. It wasn't the fear I felt when you swung for my head and missed. And it wasn't any great revelation I had on my own. It was a combination of getting you so upset that all you could do was punch me - you never tried to hit me in anger before - and looking into your eyes seeing the disappointment and hurt I caused you.

It was as if your eyes where repeatedly asking, "Why?" I mean, in a matter of mere seconds I had a full conversation with your spirit. It said,

"Phillip. You are my nephew. I love you like a son. There is nothing I wouldn't give to you. Why would you steal from me of all people? I see so much potential inside of you but your attitude… the chip on your shoulder is going to keep you from reaching it. I don't know what to say or do to get you to change, but you have to."

From that look… that swing… and the few words you said when you walked away, I knew I had to let go. Do you even remember what you said? I do. After you swung and missed, the only thing you said to me as you walked away shaking your head was, *"You don't get it."*

Unc… I got it.

But I went through all of that to actually tell you the reason why I always wanted to wear your clothes was because you were cool. I love you Uncle Richard.

PS

I still remember the baseball game you took us to. I remember and appreciate how you would not only let me tag along when you, Rick, Jay and Rob played basketball, but how you would pick me to play no matter who was out there. And one day, I hope to have a son so I can show him how to throw a football and loop his tie the way you taught me.

From Me, to You…

Previously I spoke about the need for more males to step up and become mentors in our community. My Uncle Richard took on that role for me in certain areas of my life. More often than anyone else, you may hear me speak of my Uncle Bobby simply because we communicate on more levels than anyone else in my life. However, Uncle Richard is the one who always pushed me to be the best athlete and all around person I could be.

Though we bumped heads often when I was younger, I look back and see the lessons he often tried to teach. One thing I never told him; I learned more by watching him than listening. I loved and admired the passion he possessed while playing pickup games of basketball, probably more so than observing his natural skill on the court. Hearing the comments people made about him on the sideline seemed to have embodied sincere respect for who my uncle was. That is important to me.

People may admire you for your abilities and many talents. Whether it is how fast you run, how high you jump or the manner in which you may speak, and how you carry yourself around others. Yet admiration, much like fear, doesn't always produce respect. People not only admired my Uncle Richard but they respected his game. He was always one of the best and hardest workers on the court but he never boasted about his abilities. He lifted other people up and got them involved to try and make them better. I learned it is not always about how well you play, but how well can you make those around you play. That is the measure of a true leader.

One additional lesson I learned that is closely related; anyone can boast about themselves and hype their own skills up to sound like the best. But the question is; what do other people say about you when you are not there to hear them? Usually, I would be the first to say, "never concern yourself with what others think of you", but the reality

From Me, to You…

is, a person's perception of you does matter. Always strive to live a life that evokes more good than bad.

I hope these lessons I learned from Uncle Richard help you in some area of your life as well.

"God gave you two ears and one mouth. You need to use them in that proportion." –Unknown

Hi Aunt Diane,

Thank you again for all the food you and Momma cooked for my birthday party. As you could tell everyone simply loved it. When I look back on my life and the times we have shared, two things come to mind; no nonsense and great food.

I don't know if you remember this, but once when I was about five years old, I was walking to school with Momma. I think we lived on San Juan at the time. Well, while we were walking she got angry with me about something and for a minute she started to raise her voice. When she did, I can recall beginning to cry because I was afraid I was going to get a whooping. Instead of giving me a whooping, Momma apologized for yelling at me and gave me a hug.

The very next morning, I did something I wasn't supposed to and you started yelling at me. Thinking back to what happened the day before, I quickly thought I would drum up some fake tears and get a little sympathy again. I'll never forget looking up at you from the bottom of those stairs…

"Boy what is wrong with you!?"

"You yelled at me!"

And with that I thought I was about to get a great big hug…

"I'M GONE DO MORE THAN YELL AT YO LITTLE BEHIND IF YOU DON'T DO WHAT I TOLD YOU TO!"

I remember thinking, *'she don't give a damn!'*

That is Auntie Diane. In a lot of ways you remind me of Gran'moan. You don't raise your voice often or even get upset. But when you do, who ever is on the other end of that anger, better watch out. And just like Gran'moan, I see how you express your love for the family through your cooking.

I will always remember how you and Tim took care of me when I came to visit in New Orleans. Maaaan… that smothered chicken, rice & gravy and home style biscuits! Then to top it all off, Tim got me drunk as a skunk. That was the first time I ever had homemade corn liquor. Tasted like rubbing alcohol. But as you know that didn't stop us. I had a great time. We had a great time.

I just wanted to share those few thoughts with you and tell you that I love you. I still want to help turn the dream of our family owning a restaurant into a reality. We'll talk more later.

Phillip

*"It's not the size of the dog in the fight that matters. It's the size of the fight in the dog." –**Unknown***

Dear Uncle Kevin,

Reading the poem, *"After a While"* from your obituary on Gran'moan's porch, was at that time, the most difficult thing I ever had to do. You were the first person close to me that passed away. I looked forward to hearing you come through the door almost every afternoon. "Phillip Mozelle The Most… Grasshopper the Third!"

Damn this is really hard right now…

That was the nickname you gave me. If you didn't call me that, you just called me, "Phillip Carradine the Second." I loved how you would come over to sit and talk with me and Gran'moan. I enjoyed listening to everything you had to say. It didn't matter whether it was a card trick, a funny joke or stories about how you grew up. To this day I still remember the story of The 'Signified Monkey from Dolemite', because of you. Every time I share that poem, either with the guys from my football team or while simply playing cards with friends…they all fall out laughing…You always kept a smile on my face.

I loved when we would go for ice cream. You would always joke about the two of us while sitting under a tree in the shade, hiding from the sun. *"Grasshopper, we need to just get us some ice cream cones, find us a tree and lay under it like fat rats… then after we finish, we'll let the ice cream drip on the side of our mouth, rub on our bellies and just holla… Wooooooeeeeeee!"* I crack up laughing to myself every time I think about that. It was so easy for me to see exactly what everybody else saw in you. I don't know if I ever told you, but everyone got pretty excited about you moving back to Michigan; I learned a different story about your life almost every day. One I'll never forget is about how you got the nickname Hawkeye…

When you all lived in New Orleans during the 60's, Momma said, you and Uncle John use to fight a lot. She told me about the fight you got into, when you were living in the projects, that changed your life.

One of the kids pulled out a knife and stabbed you in the eye. Hearing and even writing about that story makes me cringe. I don't know how that would have affected me; from what I hear, having a glass eye didn't slow you down one bit. The way Momma puts it, *"Kevin is gone be Kevin."* She said, another time you were with a group of friends and you got into a fight with one of them. I can't remember if the boy pushed or punched you. Whatever the case was, afterwards he ran around the corner. Instead of running after him, Momma said, you picked up a brick and threw it between two houses and hit the guy in the head. Now if that aint a Hawkeye, I don't know what is. I guess she was right, nothing could stop you.

Our family also told me about how you were scouted by a Semi-pro football team, after moving to California with Gran'moan's sister, Auntie Robin, in 1972. You must have been super fast! Uncle John told me you use to hustle people by betting that you could win a race on foot against them, while you were running backwards. The crazy thing was… you really could! I was convinced when you beat me the same way. What surprised me the most about the football story, was how they didn't know you had a glass eye? To think; if you didn't have to take that physical exam, my Uncle would have walked onto a team and possibly played in the NFL after dropping out of high school. I use to get excited just picturing you out there running like Earl

Campbell. I knew you had to be tough. But the incident in Indiana taught me just how much you loved the family, and to what lengths you would go to protect us all.

The rest of the family relocated to Indiana, when you moved to California. Uncle Bobby said you would visit them from time to time whenever you got a chance. This particular time you flew out in '74. Gran'moan was here in Detroit looking for a place for the family to live, so she had you look after everything.

The day before she returned, Uncle Bobby told me a boy took his bike from him while at the store. He said, when he came home to tell you about it, you walked him around the corner where the boy was and made them fight. Uncle Bobby won, took his bike back, and the both of you went back home. I guess I would have thought that was the end of it too. But you must have known something was going to happen; you tucked a knife under your sleeve before you went out to talk to the boy's older brother. Momma said the only reason why they knew where Uncle Bobby lived, was because he and the boy went to the same school.

I never knew until recently what exactly happened to make you stab the guy in the chest, right in the front yard. Uncle Richard told me there were two other guys, the little boy, and a girl sitting in the car. At some point during the conversation, the girl screamed out for the older brother to shoot you. He never saw the knife, and you were much too fast for him to pull the gun.

Momma says after you stabbed him, the guy started shooting and managed to catch you in the side. As they shot at the house, you somehow made it in through the side door without being hit again. After you checked on everyone to make sure they were safe, Uncle Bobby said, *"He ran out the side door again while they were still shooting… jumped into the car and stabbed three out of the five, leaving two people dead."*

That very next day the family moved to Detroit to get away from the local media attention that this incident attracted.

The outcome of that incident was horrible, and in no way should it be glorified. But, if I may speak from the heart, when I hear that story, I think of a hero, a protector, a man who loved his family. Someone threatened your family and you risked your own life to protect them. As a young man then and even now, I don't see that lesson being taught much anymore. A lot of our men today don't seem to want that role. But what amazed me the most, was after hearing all the stories about the fighting, the stealing and the drugs; when you moved here in 85', you never let us see that side of you.

If anyone were to ask me, who Uncle Kevin was, I'd say, "Uncle Kevin was the greatest guy in the world. He loved his family more than he loved himself." I remember once we were sitting in the living room talking. Somehow we got on the subject of religion, and I asked if you believed in God. You said something much more profound, something I only could have hoped to have understood back then…"*I do believe in God. But I don't just see God as some great being in the sky. I see God in people.*"

Despite any of the things you did, that would be seen as sinful or bad, I saw God in you, a lot more now than what I did when I was younger. I saw God's loving and protecting hand, through the way you cared for us. Sometimes I wished I was older in age, just so I could have been there to protect you. I wish I could have made you follow your doctor's orders. Now that I think about it; no one could make Unc do anything. Not even the doctor that tried to regulate your diet after you were placed on dialysis. I wish I knew you were still struggling. Maybe I could have stood up and told you how much I loved you, and didn't want to see you hurt yourself. But I was a young man, and didn't understand what you were going through.

I'll never forget that morning back in '92. Auntie Ellen called the house late and said you were in the hospital. You were in a car accident, after falling asleep at the wheel. She said you must have been tired from your dialysis. Momma and everyone rushed out as fast as they could. I stayed home to watch all of the kids. "*God please make sure he is ok. Please, take care of my Uncle*", was all I could pray for at that time. And though I prayed that prayer, the thought of you not coming home, never entered my mind. *"Unc is going to be fine, that's Unc,"* is what I told myself.

So it didn't seem strange when Aunt Jackie called back less than an hour later to say you were fine, and they were on the way back home. While I felt some relief, in my mind I already knew you were going to be ok.

It was about 5:30am when the door opened. I was lying down in Gran'moans room. Even though people were walking in, for the most part it was silent. I could hear a faint sound in the distance slowly getting louder. At first it sounded like laughter, followed by mumbling.

"I-got-bro-moe". Then a split second of silence.

Now the laughs were getting closer... I couldn't make out the voice so I rolled out of bed and walked into the hallway.

"I-done-got-bro-moe!... PHILLIP!!!!"

It was Momma... she wasn't laughing at all. She was crying...

"PHILLIP!!! I DON'T GOT NO BROTHER NO MORE!!!!!"

As I quickly reached out to hold her, Uncle Richard followed behind us to tell me what happened.

"Man, Uncle Kevin's kidney collapsed and he died in there." Then Momma's voice screamed mercifully over us all...

"HOLD ME PHILLIIIIP! HOLD MEEEEE!!!! MY BROTHER GONE!!!!"

As much as I wanted to cry I couldn't. Not at that moment. I knew I had to be strong for Momma. I couldn't help but think, *"How...*

From Me, to You…

Not my hero…. Not Hawk Eye. The same man who survived being stabbed in the eye as a kid! The same man who could beat people running backward while they ran forward! Not Unc!"

It didn't fully hit me until I had to walk down that isle, and I saw you laying in that coffin. With every step, the lump in my throat got bigger and the tears flowed faster. I finally realized there would be no more Dolomite stories. No more afternoon games of Tunk, Spades or Domino's. I would never again hear you say, "Grasshopper, fix me one of them Dagwood's". Who would go and get ice cream with me!? Who would I sit under the tree with… make my belly full… lay back and just say…

"OH GOD I MISS YOU UNC!!!!!!!"

I love you just as much today as I did when you were here. No matter what type of lifestyle you had outside of home, you never exposed your family to it. You loved us with all you had to give. You are the definition of a protector. I love you, and I thank God for what little time we had. May the Lord continue to hold you close in His loving arms.

Until the trumpet sounds,

Phillip Mozelle The Most… Grasshopper the Third

by Phil Black

From Me, to You…

"Brothers, we do not want you to be ignorant about those who fall asleep, or to grieve like the rest of men, who have no hope. We believe that Jesus died and rose again and so we believe that God will bring with Jesus those who have fallen asleep in him. According to the Lord's own word, we tell you that we who are still alive, who are left till the coming of the Lord, will certainly not precede those who have fallen asleep. For the Lord himself will come down from heaven, with a loud command, with the voice of the archangel and with the trumpet call of God, and the dead in Christ will rise first. After that, we who are still alive and are left will be caught up together with them in the clouds to meet the Lord in the air. And so we will be with the Lord forever. Therefore encourage each other with these words."

-1 Thessalonians 4:13-18 NIV

Death is a part of life we must all experience in some way. My first experience was with the death of a fifth grade classmate who was the victim of a hit and run accident. I recall feeling a sense of sorrow for his family, and even fear for my own life. The thought of being here one day and gone the next had not entered my mind. Yet with the passing of my Uncle Kevin, that same thought took on a new and personal definition.

When people who have impacted our lives suddenly disappear, we find it difficult to deal with the reality of never seeing them again. How they dressed, the way they walked, the sound of their voice or even the warmth of their touch, suddenly becomes our souls desire. Just one more time, one more conversation, or one more laugh. One more hug. One more opportunity to say I love you. These thoughts consumed me as well, and still do from time to time. However, today I have a better understanding that comforts me through those times.

The old saying is true, "people are brought into your life for a reason and a season." God allows us to experience His love and nature through them. From the beginning of time we were all given a course and a calling. Your calling is simply how the Lord introduces Himself to others through you. Your course is the path that you must travel to reach that calling. Along the way God places certain people in our lives to help teach and train us as we grow in the maturity of His ways.

My Uncle Kevin brought joy into the hearts of many. He was a living example of love and protection for me to follow. Though I miss him dearly and wished we had that "one more time" together, I find comfort in portraying the lessons I learned from his life. As a result, he lives on through me each time I pass on one of his messages. Mourning the loss of another is never easy. But celebrating their life should come with grace. We never know when our seasons with one another will end. Make it a point to enjoy your life with others, as much as you can, for as long as you can.

From Me, to You…

"The separation from Good to Great has a distance of only six letters…
DESIRE." –PB

To the shoulder I needed,

I truly wish I remembered your name. Mine is Phil Black. I'm sure you don't remember me or even know why I am writing you. During the summer of 1994, three of my teammates and I, from Highland Park High School, came to The University Michigan for the annual five day summer football camp. You were a student there at the time and working as the hall monitor on our floor. I never really had an opportunity to share with you how I got there or why their words bothered me so much.

My entire life I dealt with people making jokes about my skin color or whatever they could think of. It caused me to be very insecure for a long time. Over the years I got really good at football. Not because I just had a lot of raw skill, in fact I wasn't very fast or even the biggest; it was because I would try my best to work harder than anyone else, that's why I did well.

From nine years of age until I moved away for college, I would run around the neighborhood once, even sometimes twice a day. The entire route was about four miles. I would work out with the cement weights my Uncle Richard gave me or at the Power Gym down the street, as I had gotten older. Even as a freshman I would always jump ahead of everyone to be the first in line for all the drills. I was never afraid to compete against the number one guy in any of the four sports I played in High School. I developed this, "you have to beat me" mentality. It mostly came from the anger I had inside, fueled by the many jokes people told about me. I felt like I could get the last laugh by beating them. I truly believe that the mental toughness I acquired from all of the pain is what brought me so far. The reason why I loved playing football so much was because out there on the field, I was in control. Guys could say what they wanted to about me out there; it didn't matter because we both knew they had to line up against me at some point.

I only wanted to play defense because I could take out any pain or frustration I was feeling. If I got into an argument or someone said something negative to me in school (which was usually guys on the team) I'd just reply by saying, "Wait til we strap up." There was one problem with that ...we didn't walk around in pads during everyday life, which is why when Ken and Anthony began to talk about me during camp, there was nothing I could do. It wasn't that I couldn't tell jokes at the time. The reason it hurt so bad was because they didn't come across as jokes at all.

"Nigga you aint shit! I mean you got the gloves, the wrist bands, visor and sweet ass face mask... but you aint shit!"

In broad daylight, walking from the dorms to the football field; hundreds of other players from across the country, attended the camp were walking by laughing, shaking their heads in disbelief. Except Marcus, he was the starting quarterback for our rival school.

"Phil, why are those guys talking about you like that? Aren't they on your team?"

"Supposed to be." I replied.

From Me, to You…

"Dude don't listen to them. You're going to do good this season."

As hurtful and embarrassing as that moment turned out to be, it wasn't until the end of the night, while in my dorm room, that I realized, these guys were not joking with me at all.

When I came out to talk with you, I was ready to cry my heart out. To make jokes or talk about someone in a teasing manner for the sake of entertaining others with a laugh is one thing, but when the ridicule continues when an audience isn't around is another. You are only left to believe that the jokes are not jokes, but yet a true perception of what is thought of you. Even though you didn't say much, you made me feel better just by listening. And I am happy to say, I had my best season ever as a senior.

I finished with 108 tackles, 40 of them solo, 12 of them for a loss, 6 forced fumbles, 3 fumble recoveries, 2 interceptions and 4 touchdowns (without ever playing offense). After the season I was nominated first team All Conference, Second Team All City and Honorable mention for all others, including All State. I never told anyone, but I thought about that camp and that night before every game. And I want to say thank you, for being the shoulder I needed.

Phil Black

by Phil Black

From Me, to You…

*"As long as we are on this side of the ground, we have a chance." –**Miss Gladis***

Dear Uncle Bobby,

When I decided to write this letter to you, a part of me wanted to focus on the many ways you have contributed to my life. You stepped in and surpassed the expectations of an uncle, and treated me like a son. And for that, I cannot say thank you enough. I become somewhat emotional when I allow myself to think about you; the only thing I can do is smile.

There have been times I have dialed your number or visited your home, all worked up over a situation that had been proven to be beyond my control, and you, with such an amazing grace, would put me at ease. Before I would even reveal my troubles, you would have something humorous or witty to say, or even a simple, but yet profound quote. It seemed like your words always came right on time. In most cases I'd either forget what was bothering me or realized it wasn't as bad as it seemed. From that, I have learned the value of not putting so much pressure on myself.

For years I have always interacted with people, and attacked life as if it were a chess match, trying to stay at least three to four moves ahead; while at the same time attempting to read everyone who sat across the table. I admire the way you simply allow people to be themselves, while governing your own actions, rather than trying to control theirs.

Every time I have tried to monitor someone else's behavior, out of my own insecurities, I still wound up seeing the outcome I was hoping to avoid. I'll never forget the joke you told, to teach me that lesson...

"There was this dog... very well groomed and attractive. The thing people were drawn to the most was his tail. Now, this dog's tail was beautiful. Long and fluffy. The most beautiful tail you could imagine on a dog. It was so beautiful because the dog took excellent care of it. He would wash, blow dry, brush and trim it every day; sometimes two or three times. One day this dog was walking across a set of train tracks as a train was coming. Just before the train got to him he made it on the other side. But as he looked back, his tail was still on the track. So the dog turned around real quick to reach back for his beautiful tail. The second he turned around the train came and took his head clean off."

The moral is this...

I don't care how pretty it is... don't loose yo' head over no tail."

Who couldn't feel that story? I know I did. I have lost my head before, more times than I'd like to remember. Trying to invest more into others then what they were willing to invest in me. I was so unhappy inside. As you know, for years I went from relationship to relationship. Recently a friend of mine jokingly said, *"Phil Black loves, love."* As true as that statement is (and I see nothing wrong with loving others), I think what he observed was how I had a tendency to give up everything for anyone who chose me. Which is very true. For a long time I wanted to be loved so much, that I had a "just add Phil and mix" approach to selecting a mate. It didn't matter who it was, as long as they gave off the appearance of caring for me.

I do feel you must be giving and loving toward someone who deserves your love; however, you cannot lose you in the process -

From Me, to You…

Which is yet another lesson I learned from you. I know you say that you are not a scholar; but Uncle Bobby, no one would be able to tell. That's why I was so shocked and moved to learn that you didn't know how to read until you were almost 13. To this day, you are one of the most knowledgeable people I have ever met.

You have helped me realize how valuable and precious life is; how it is possible to miss out on its' beauty without even knowing it. I remember you saying…

"I enjoy my job and what it provides for me and my family. But at the end of the day it's just a job. I can get another one. I can't get another you."

It has taken me the past five to ten years to truly understand the lesson those words embodied, although it took time and experience to learn what you meant, you never gave up on me. And you have continued to bless me with your knowledge and wisdom.

There was something else you taught me…

"Two drowning people can't save each other. Someone has to get out first in order to reach back and save the other."

Your actions showed me exactly what you meant; you have always been able and willing to reach back, but you always manage to maintain balance in your life.

You told me once…

"It's just not that deep. I give them the best work I can offer for the time I am there. But when I punch out on the clock, I punch out in my mind too…..I am not going to give up my life building someone else's dream"

This has always been one of the more difficult lessons for me to put into action. I was so focused on being successful and moving up the ladder; I couldn't imagine not thinking about what had to be done the next day, month or even the next minute. Actually the first time you said those words to me, I viewed that as a negative statement. I felt like, what choice do I have, if I want to succeed.

"I have to work this job as if it were my own company, if I want to move ahead," was the mentality I had. To some degree I still feel that way and not just for myself. If your goal is to move up the corporate ladder, the only way to do it is to take ownership of the position you are in. View everything through a big picture lense. Learn not only how to perform the duties of your position, and the one in front of you; but also, learn how to teach and train others to do what you do. That has always been my secret.

Although this concept on succession has been beneficial to my life – at this moment – my outlook has taken a new course… Progression is success in its own right, but significance as an individual is just as rewarding. It is just a matter of defining what significant means to you. This also, is a lesson I have learned by observing you in action.

Uncle Bobby, you deal with everyone you touch from a pure heart. You are straight up and hold no punches. When people ask me for my advice a lot of times I will use your disclaimer;

"You can choose to take all of it, some of it or none of it."

Your words and actions have taught me so much, from how you have supported me, and continue to do so, in everything that I do, to how you now participate in the success of your own children. You are able to give us all that you can, without taking away from yourself.

I heard you talking to my cousins, and somehow directing your attention to me as well…

From Me, to You…

"At the end of the day, daddy got to be happy too. So I take mine off the top. After I take care of the business and hand some of it out, we can party with the rest. But once that's gone, it's gone. I never go in my back pocket."

You have shown more intelligence than most, simply through how you live. The quotes and humor are a bonus. I just thank you for being so giving of the knowledge you possess and more importantly the time. People sometimes ask me did I miss not having my father around. I did at times, from the standpoint of desiring to spend time with the actual man who helped create me. But when I combine all that I have received from the family and you specifically; I can say I have always had a father, someone who took me to ballgames, cookouts, fishing, road trips or just out on the porch to talk.

So this letter is just a thank you, and a celebration of the man you are and the man you have helped me to become. I love you.

Your son

PS

"I will always have money for a sandwich."

From Me, to You…

I obviously recognize more today, the blessing I had in the midst of my storms. Society would have you to believe that there are no good men left, and that there is no possible way to create anymore. I may be way off base or just speaking from my usual "love to love" mindset, but I think they are wrong.

Not only do I believe we have some strong, would be role models and mentors amongst us; I think they are ready to stand up and be counted. The problem I see is no different from what we have dealt with as children. Have you ever sat in a classroom and had a question about a lesson but for fear of looking and sounding dumb you refused to raise your hand? Then moments later someone else becomes bold enough to ask the very same question? Later, you find that almost everyone in the class were just as confused?

I believe some of our men are stagnated due to the fear of judgment and ridicule. I think many of us have the same desire for change in our hearts. Look at the overwhelming impact made on our society through the election of the first African American President, Barak Obama. While it was and is a great moment for the image of the black male in particular, the idea of being a Harvard graduate and becoming President of the United States for many, still seems to be a star just too far to reach.

Taking a quote from Bill Cosby's book, Come On, People;

"No matter how useless or hopeless a father may think he is, his role is simply to be there. If he makes that commitment, he is a much better man than he thought of himself to be."

You do not have to be the next President, although you could be. You do not have to be the next Lebron James, yet with hard work and dedication you just may be. Now more than ever our society needs more everyday men to stand up and say no more.

No more, will we allow the excuses. No more will we live in fear of our young. No more, will we allow our women to be degraded as pieces of meat on the auction block. It amazes me how almost every other culture in America besides the African American culture are so protective of their women and children.

Am I saying that I am perfect? In no way! Am I saying that my Uncle Bobby or anyone else I have highlighted are perfect examples of manhood? Not at all, although many of these men, in their own right, were effective role models for me, but what I am saying is each one individually provides "an example." To the men of our time, Stand up…We need you.

From Me, to You…

"You can't whoop everybody…" –**Kenneth M. Black**

Dear Daryl,

What's been good brother? I pray all is well with you.

I am writing you in response to the message you sent me via the Internet. As you know, at the time I was at a loss for words. Your note touched me so much that the only thing I could do was break out in tears. Do you remember what you wrote? I do…

"What's up Phil? Your talk about going out had me thinking about a night I'll never forget where I was struggling on whether I should go to a party or not. I wanted to tell you this a long time ago and never got the chance. I contemplated going to that frat party where you had the unfortunate incident years ago. I knew how I was raised but I wasn't trying to live for the Lord at the time. So I decided to go and had a lot of fun, and then the incident happened. What made the night memorable for me is seeing you bent over and realizing why I had went to the party. I wasn't a bold person but I did ease over and laid my hand on you for a second and prayed to God to keep and protect you. I saw you a while later at Wayne State and the Lord told me to tell you He had a plan for your life and that He would use your leadership skills for Him. When I saw you that day at Wayne State I said I had to holler at you but after that day I never saw you again until bowling for our ten year. So today I'm happy but not surprised to see you being bold about your faith. God

bless you man and the sky is the limit for what you can do for Christ. Take it easy and holler back."

Daryl, even as I sit here attempting to write to you my eyes are welling up. Brother I can't tell you how much those words… your prayer… the fact that God sent you to that particular party, at that time in space, means to me. It is funny how divine order works, because I also thought about staying home that night…

As you know, it was Homecoming Weekend, September 27, 1997. After the game all of the guys on the team asked if I would hang out with them down at The Forest (The main apartment building on campus at the time where most athletes lived). I told them I might go, but I wasn't sure. At the time I lived off campus at my Grandmother's house back in Highland Park. I was actually awarded an apartment in The Forest that semester as part of my scholarship. I just never moved in. I still don't know why I was so uncomfortable about being around everyone on a regular basis back then.

I went directly home after we left the stadium, and later that night my mother called me on the phone from work, and asked if I planned to go out. I told her no because I was tired and a little sore from the game, but after we hung up I got into the mood for a drink. So I walked to the store and got a 40oz. It didn't take long after I finished it, and any reservations I had about going to The Forest disappeared. I caught the Woodward bus down there around 9 or 9:30pm. Everyone was in Jay and Fred's room. I say room because The Forest was built more like a dorm than an apartment building.

There were about six guys from the team and a few girls from the hoop squad already there. When I say they welcomed me with open arms… man, they showed me much love.
I remember Jay saying, *"You acted like you was allergic to The Forest."* I guess I didn't hide my apprehension as well as I thought I did. Nonetheless, we kicked it as if I was a regular. It felt as if I had been apart of the football team for YEARS! We talked. We drank. We

Laughed. We drank! We Screamed. We Drank!... Did I mention we drank?

That was the night I was introduced to 'Ray'. Franklin called it the budget Cognac. (I don't know about that, but I do know it does the deed). We hung out at the apartment until almost 11 o'clock. After about three more beers and at least four shots I was nice and tipsy. Since I didn't have a car I think I road with Tom and Corey T. Who's ever car it was I do remember Corey being with me. I knew Corey before I transferred to Wayne State. So I was pretty comfortable going to the party with everyone, even though I was the only Que on campus at the time.

I had just crossed back in April of the same year. I'm not sure if you have ever encountered a Neophyte Que fresh out of his undergraduate experience; if you haven't let me tell you, I was a bit of a handful, to say the least. It was routine for me to wake up singing frat songs to myself, and that would continue while in the shower and while dressing myself for the day; which usually consisted of some type of purple ripped or sleeveless shirt, cammy green shorts, some type of army hat, my spiked dog color (equipped with a five foot purple leash), my purple book bag (that I kept my gold, three foot long dog bone in) and of course The Gold Boots.

It was normal for me to get so amped in the morning, that by the time I made it to the Union I just couldn't take it anymore. The only thing I could do to express my fervor and excitement for being apart of the best fraternity, was to set out a Hop! And that I did, right in the middle of the Union. In front of students, faculty, administrators… it didn't matter. I just couldn't contain my love for the Bruhz. I didn't care if I was the only one there beside Goldie (who had already graduated and was now working in the Financial Aid office). What I didn't realize at the time Daryl, was that while a lot of people enjoyed seeing me express myself and were drawn to the genuine love I displayed; there were also a lot of people who were intimidated by me as well. Back then I was somewhat aware, but I did not truly understand the potential implications of it.

When we got to the party it was almost 11:30pm. You would think it was prime party time. But Daryl, like a comedian I once heard said… *"There weren't enough people there to start a rumor."* And you know what? That was all the ammo I needed to start talking trash to the guy's that threw the party.

"Are you serious?" "Are YOU serious?" "This is why don't nobody like ya'll!" "What Hammer say? 'YO PARTY WASN'T JUMPIN AND YO DJ WAS WEAK!"

I was cutting a stone cold fool from the minute I walked in the door. Again, I didn't know any better and I was being me. In my mind it was all in fun. In fact, after one of my trash talking sessions I took one of the guys and taught him how to tap the keg. That was my way of showing Greek love. Of course it didn't come free. They had to hear about that too.

"Ya'll can't tap a damn keg either? DAMN! I thought ya'll were MEN!?"

I know… I know… I was trippin. But it was funny. I had almost everybody rolling all night. I had to do something to entertain myself until the crowd got there or at least a few more women, which did happen not long after. But that still didn't calm me down.

I remember dancing with a girl while the DJ played one of my favorite songs. It got me kind of amped, so I started barking. Within seconds one of the Ice-men who threw the party walked up to me,

"Dude I'm getting tired of you… this ain't a Que party!"

So how did I respond? The only way a young, buck wild Neo would…

"FUCK-YOU… I'M A MUTHA-FUCKIN QUE!" And with that I started barkin' in his face.

From Me, to You…

We got into a short pushing match but before anything happened, Corey, a few guys on the squad and some of the guys there came and broke it up. Later that night me and the guy made up the way guys do;

"It's too many females in here for us to be fightin' bro!"

"That's what I'm talkin' about."

About fifteen minutes after that, this guy I use to know from Eastern came up to me and Corey.

"What up Black? Aye, we got some dancers upstairs. Ya'll need to come check 'em out."

"Alright." After he walked off we kept dancing with the girls we were with.

"You know that dude?" Corey asked.

"Yeah. He went to Eastern. We aint cool like that though."

"Oh, you want to go check it out upstairs?"

"Not right now, I'll come in a minute."

After a few more songs the girl I was dancing with said she was getting hot and stepped outside to get a little air.

"That's cool. I'll meet up with you in a few."

"Ok."

When she left to go outside I decided to make a trip up the stairs. Why not? It's been all of twenty minutes and Corey hasn't come back down so it must have been live.

When I got to the top of the narrow stair case, there was a table blocking anyone from simply walking through. There was one guy standing next to it and another sitting down to collect money.

"Fifteen." He said.

"Fifteen what?"

"Fifteen dollars to get in."

"Dude, my mans didn't say nothing about no fifteen dollars. I'm gone wait for my boy Tony, he threw this party to."

I stood there for a few more minutes. People were walking past to get in and out. Reflecting back, I have to admit, it was a bit of a tight squeeze with me standing there. But the guy playing security didn't say that. All he said was,

"You gotta go downstairs!" As he said it he reached out to force me by the arm. I retaliated by slapping his hand away.

"Dude, don't touch me."

"You gotta go!"

"Why!? I can't see shit! Ya'll got the doors closed! My boy gone be up here in a minute, chill out!" But while I was speaking the second guy stood up too.

"You GOTTA GO NOW!"

From Me, to You…

Together they pushed me and I stumbled almost to the bottom of the stairs. By the time I gathered myself, a small crowd of people were around me. The two guys from up stairs, the guy I was arguing with earlier, Tony and his boys, Larry and Jeff from Eastern, and two other guys I didn't even know.

We were arguing and pushing at each other, along with another guy acting as security, all the while, Tony was trying to break it up. I can't remember why, but as if necessary, Tony walked away. As soon as he left one of them swung and hit me. IT WAS ON! We ALL were fighting… or should I say they were ALL fighting me. Even though I was completely drunk, the adrenaline mixed with my football conditioning allowed me to hold my own. They couldn't get any good punches on me or take me down, so they collectively rushed me, and force me out of the side door. It worked. But this is the point where a bad night got worse. I remember thinking to myself,

"They only doing this because I'm the only bruh here! FUCK-THEM! I aint no hoe!"

When I said that; I made my way around the house, went through the front door, wove my way through the crowd, went back through the kitchen, rounded the corner leading to the small area where the altercation started… and started fighting again. We went at it for another two to three minutes before I heard one of them say,

"Nigga you still in here tryin to be tough! YOU DON'T SEE ALL THESE GUNS ON YOU NIGGA!?"

I turned to my right and was staring into the barrel of a pistol. Never turning to see what was to my left I stopped and surrendered. To show that I had given up, I went to both knees, turned my palms to the sky with my elbows tucked to my side and bowed my head. The next thing I heard through the commotion was,

*"DOG! DOG!... DON'T SHOOT DAT NIGGA! I'LL BE RIGHT BACK!"*And like I said Daryl... I never even looked to the left. I didn't think I had to.

"BANG!"

I saw a light flash off the floor and my head jerked to the right. I was so drunk I thought I had gotten punched. In that split second I remember thinking,

"I'm not gone let you just whoop my ass! Gun or no Gun!" So I tried to stand up...

"BANG!"

I felt the second shot hit my forearm. I must have lost a lot of blood from my face because, I remember falling down. I had to have only blacked out for a few seconds; because the next thing I heard was,

"OH! NIGGA YOU STILL FUCKIN' MOVIN!?"

"BANG!"

I never even felt that one graze the back of my head.

Lying in that pool of blood... blacking in and out... hearing the screams... the crying... it all felt like a dream. Finally I heard voices I could recognize. It was Corey and Jay.

"Phil!?"

"Phil!?"

"Phil!?"

From Me, to You…

"Lord PLEASE!"

"Phil!?"

"Dog, if you can hear me say something! Do something! ANYTHING!"

So I did…

      I felt so special when everyone came to see me at the hospital. I really didn't know how to receive it. The cards, the flowers, the stuffed dogs, the Superman hat… everything. At that very moment I knew God had people watching over me. I knew there were people out there praying for me. So when you sent me that note…

      When you sent me that note, it just reminded me of how much God does and has always loved me. Daryl M., you served as part of His legion of angels that night. I love you brother. I thank and Bless God for you, and everyone else who came to my aid. Who knows if you were not there at that time to say that prayer, I may not have made it. Thank you.

Your Brother,

Phil

Dear Dr. Evan,

I recently wrote a letter to a friend of mine who attended the party I got shot at back in '97 and of course, I thought of you. That night was a mess. I barely remember the drive to the hospital let alone getting admitted. I do remember lying on the gurney, throwing up the hooks. I was so wasted, I couldn't tell if I was asleep or if this was really happening. I remember lying there for a long time, cold and bleeding. After a while I began to wonder if anyone would come. Did they even care that I was lying there and could possibly die? So when you walked over to me and whispered in my ear, I couldn't help but to break out into tears.

When you wheeled me into the room I thought my life was almost over. But when you pinched my nipples hard enough to take them off I knew it wasn't. By the way that stuff hurt man. I want to thank you for keeping your word. Your oath to both the medical profession and Omega.

No one can ever tell me that God does not exist and that He does not have a divine order that is to be - and will be - carried out. What are the odds... on THAT day... at THAT exact time... a young man who decided to pledge an organization back in 1991 and pursue a career that would prove to save the lives of others... would meet another young man who made the same decision to enter the same organization six years later in that hallway!?

I truly believe, if you were not there... I would have died! But God sent you.

Thank you Brother Evan, I could never repay you.

Phil Black

From Me, to You...

Dear Corey T.,

Team... I know we don't talk as much as we should or use to, but please don't ever think for a minute that I don't humbly thank and appreciate you coming to my aid like you did. It still puts me in awe when I think about how you picked me up and carried me into the police car that night. If we waited for the ambulance there is no telling what would have happened. (Damn you got me crying again)...

The way you kept me in the back of that car... talking... singing...just being there.

What do you say?

Thank you friend... Thank you.

JUL

U-M coach Lloyd Carr wants tailbacks such as s● above, to break more tackles and awaken the ru●

homecoming

BY GEORGE SIPPLE
Free Press Sports Writer

College is a place where memories are made. And every year, the homecoming football game gives alumni a chance to relive their memories.

But when Wayne State hosts Ashland for homecoming at 1 p.m. today, sophomore linebacker Phil Black would rather forget what happened to him last year.

Black, 21, was involved in a skirmish hours after playing in his first Wayne State homecoming game last Sept. 27, a 46-30 loss to Grand Valley State. He was shot at close range in the face and elbow, and missed the rest of the season.

Black, who transferred to Wayne from Eastern Michigan shortly after the season began, said he had left a gathering of teammates and attended an off-campus party around 11:30 p.m.

During the party he was told female dancers were on the second

Phil Black

Starting with runnii U-M needs widespre

WOLVERINES, from Page 1B

themselves. Losing, nose tackle Rob Renes said, would be "potentially devastating."

"I certainly think Michigan State will be the biggest test of the season for us," coach Lloyd Carr said, "because I think we're going to find out where we are in terms of what kind of a team we can have."

To win, the Wolverines will have to do several things well, and that means improving across the board:

■ U-M must win the rushing battle. History is quite clear on this: In 28 of

conversion back Tom because of

Unlike 1 running ga short oppo often have 1 have neede to convert 1 more yards 31 (22.5 per

"When Brady said, and then yo get that all s

On defen

Detroit News, September 1998

Nicks and ●. Pur- ●t. st set is and ●e on ● de- ●— for — ●nsive ry er- y is in

1-2, 1- o 0-3,

●nazoo. ●lama-

– WR FB io — ●hn- nee), l LB

ck Kar- ●ve ool's ●eds ●0- okfin he in ●as al- ●sh-

104

From Me, to You…

It has been revealed through my letters, that I have dealt with and overcame situations that have proven without a shadow of a doubt that God is real, but the night of September 27, 1997 was my time of confirmation. There truly is a God.

The shooter (who to this day has never been identified) was standing less than a foot away from me. Not one single bullet; from three attempts, touched bone. Some could jokingly argue he just had horrible aim. I would suggest not. I do not care how inexperienced you are with shooting a nine millimeter pistol; anyone can hit a target nine inches away from the barrel. So, my question is why? Why would God step in and allow my life here on earth, to be prolonged?

At the time I was not actively participating with any particular religious group. I hardly if ever attended any church. My knowledge of the Word had the depth of a five year old; and based on the story I just told I am sure you can see, I did not always treat people as nicely as I could have. So why was my life spared? I choose to believe, that each of us were created for a specific purpose and called to be a specific thing. The election and appointment of your role and duty has nothing to do with who you are, and what you may do with regard to religion or traditions of man. The person God called you to be has everything to do with His eternal plan.

We are all pieces to His divine puzzle. We go through the trials and sufferings of the age to train us in His character and ways. As crazy as it may sound to some of you; I was shot at point blank range in the face but yet, my life was spared. This trial in my life was supposed to happen. The power of God and the truth of His love, mercy and divine order were made to manifest through this experience. That moment in my life brought about realization and today I am ok with knowing that. It has helped me realize that my life is not all about me. I am freed from the bondage of condemnation and the question of whether I am going to heaven or not.

I now know that reality of going to heaven is a result and not a goal. It results from first acknowledging that we were born into slavery under the yoke of our flesh through Adam. Secondly, we must confess our sins to God. Next must we consciously repent (or turn away) from a life of governing ourselves and turn toward a new life where our actions, and more importantly, our behavior toward each other is characterized by the example of perfect love set by Christ. Once we do that, then confess with our mouths and in our hearts that Christ not only died for our sins but He also rose again on the third day; by doing so we make ourselves available for adoption as the sons of God and become joint heirs with Christ. Heaven now becomes part of our inheritance, and not a reward we seek in exchange for earthly labor.

God allowed me to be delivered into the hands of the enemy on that night so that I may be delivered by the hands of His Son to safety. He has a plan for me. And He has a plan for you. Just stand strong. And have faith.

From Me, to You…

"I finally understand for a woman it ain't easy trying to raise a man…" –
Tupac Shakur

Momma,

The first day I came home from the hospital, I could tell you didn't want to go back to work. And I can understand why. It hurt me to see you go through the torture of having to look at your only son lying in that hospital bed covered in blood. Not knowing if I was going to live or die. I can only imagine the thoughts going through your mind. What could you have been thinking when brother Evan called you at work to say,

"Your son is here at the hospital, he has been shot."

I had just spoken to you earlier that evening and told you I was staying home for the night. I can't imagine. I guess that's why you had that look in your eyes before you left.

"I'm going to work baby, do you need anything?"

"No Momma, I'm fine."

"Why don't you go upstairs and get some rest?" You asked me.

"I'm going to take a nap, but I just want to stay here on the couch."

I don't know why. For some reason I just did not want to be upstairs. I guess part of me felt safer being able to hear what was going on, on the main floor. Even though I didn't admit it; I was still pretty shook up.

While you were at work, I thought about all sorts of things. Mainly, I replayed everything in my mind over and over again. Wondering how and why I was in this position. I remember turning the radio on for a minute and then quickly turning it off because of one of the songs being played. For a long time I couldn't bear to listen to any music that even talked about shooting. I know there are some artists out there who have been shot before and they glorify it as if it is some great feat. They showcase their wounds as if they are battle scars from the streets. I didn't feel that way at all. Lying there on the couch I couldn't help but feel insignificant. To be shot is the most dehumanizing feeling one could ever experience. Someone basically just decided that the world would be much better off if you didn't exist. As if they were looking directly into the eyes of your spirit and saying, "You serve no purpose."

So I thought... ate... cried... slept... woke up; then I did it all over again. For a while I could only sleep for about an hour at a time. If I heard any type of noise I would wake up from my body going into a sudden jerk. Even to this day I can't sleep through the night regularly.

I finally fell asleep for a while, around nine o'clock. I actually wanted to stay up so that we could talk when you got home. I figured I would hear you come in the door. If not, I'd just come and talk with you in the den after you would awake in the morning. Because of the hours you worked and how tired you normally are when you get off, I never would have expected to talk to you; let alone to wake up and see what you had done. You probably don't think that I noticed, or even realize how much you affected me that night. You have always been able to show your love for me in the simplest ways, and I love you for that. Do you remember what you did that night...

Luckily I had been able to sleep for hours without any interruptions. All of a sudden... out of nowhere my body made that violent jerk, and it woke me up. I don't know if I was dreaming of the shots fired or if there was something going on outside. It was nearly pitch black the in the living room. The only light I had was from the moon creeping through the shades and the alarm clock sitting on the coffee table no more than fifteen inches away from the couch. Once I realized nothing was going on I simply rolled over to go back to sleep.

As I turned around I happen to take a glance at the floor. It looked as if somebody laid a blanket there for me if I needed it. But as my eyes adjusted to the darkness I realized that it wasn't just a blanket, you were wrapped up in it. I didn't quite understand why you were laying there that night, and I never asked, but as I write this letter with tears rolling down my face, I imagine you coming home seeing me asleep and saying,

"My world… My world would not be better off without you. You do have a purpose. I love you. I thank God that He did not take you from me."

You love me so much that you disregarded your own comfort. You laid between that coffee table and the coach, WITHOUT EVEN MOVING IT, just to be near me; to be with me, knowing that I was safe.

My entire life you have been there for me. In the times when I was right you defended me. In the times where I was wrong, you told me. You did not allow me to make excuses for myself, and you raised me with the teaching of life lessons, which encouraged me to grow into becoming the best man that I know how to be. I wanted for nothing. When I felt like the ugliest boy in the world you made me feel like the most handsome. When I thought I couldn't, you told me I could. Although I may have missed holiday and birthday cards from my father, you made sure I didn't miss them from you. Nothing makes me feel more accomplished than to know that I have made you proud. So Momma I dedicate this book and my life to you. I love you Momma.

Stank

The week I returned from the hospital.

From Me, to You...

Now that we have connected through my story to this point, you may be wondering "why such a short letter to your mother"? Good question. In fact she asked the very same question at first glance as she read the manuscript. I attempted to give her a short answer by simply saying, "Don't think about the length of the letter. Focus on the content." So when she gave me the "whatever" look, I elaborated further; just as I will for you.

I can think of hundreds of stories and examples of how my mother affected my life, both as a child and now as an adult. In fact, her decision to provide a certain standard of living for me and her dedication to seeing me become a man of substance holds enough information to fill the pages of another book. I am thankful for all that she has done and I am appreciative for the role she continues to uphold in my life, but seeing her lying on that floor just to be near me tells the story of her undying love.

Like many of the overwhelming number of single mothers in our society, she had the choice to either take on her responsibilities or pawn them off on someone else. My mother chose to stay. In making that decision she did not simply do the bare minimum. My mother took it upon herself to do her share and fill in for my father as best as she could. Did she teach me how to throw a baseball or how to deal with issues as a man? Not directly. But she did discipline me when I needed correction. She taught me to respect my elders, others and myself. My mother showed me what hard work and no excuses meant. *"No one is going to give you anything. Nor do you deserve to have things simply handed to you. If you want something, work for it."* I have learned and continue to learn much from my mother. But she would be the first to tell you she did not raise me to be the man that I am today, though much of the foundation was laid by her.

It was not until I began to interact with older men of character that I learned what being a man was about. My Uncles were consistently involved in my life, teaching me through words and examples of how men behave. I learned discipline, humility and teamwork by playing sports. Joining my fraternity exposed me to inspiring, educated, selfless men who looked like me and shared similar backgrounds. Reading the words of those who strived for more empowered me. Gaining a strong personal relationship with God and seeking knowledge of His word transformed me. My mother is right, she did not teach me to be the man that I am. But if it had not been for her love, support, commitment and initial teaching I may not have been willing to receive the rest.

I do not love and credit my mother for playing the role of both father and mother as a single parent. On the contrary, I love, respect and admire her for being the best mother any boy or man could ask for. My mother is not perfect. We had our challenges along the way. But no matter what, at the end of the day I know she is willing to give up anything to show her love for me. Even if it means squeezing between two pieces of furniture to lie on the bare floor, in the middle of the night just to be near me.

From Me, to You…

"Everyone has something to give." -Unknown

To My Angel,

I was twenty-one years old, living on the Westside with my best friend Brian, on a street called Manor. This was during my transition from Wayne State back to Eastern Michigan after I had gotten shot. After being declared academically ineligible to play football, I was forced to sit out from school and had to find work. Down to my very last pennies – literally - I borrowed my Cousin Angie's car to go to an interview with the Casino.

After driving around for a few minutes, I finally realized the building I was supposed to be in was directly across from your parking lot. Before pulling in, I drove around once looking for a sign with a price for parking. After getting five dollars worth of gas I only had a little less than three dollars in change. So with time beginning to be an issue I had to hurry and park somewhere.

"Sir, how much does it cost?" I asked as I pulled to your booth.

You didn't say a word, you just flagged me in.

"How much is it?" I asked again when I got closer.

Again, nothing. You simply came out of the booth and directed me into a spot. When you met me as I got out of the car, I thought for sure you would send me away after you found out how much money I had.

"How much money do you have son?"

"Sir, I only have about three dollars in change... that's all."

"Why are you down here?"

"I'm here for a job interview."

"Son, do you know why God chose David?"

"No sir."

You said, *"Because he was a man of honor and integrity after His own heart."*

You continued on, *"I want you to keep that change and buy yourself something to eat. You are going to walk in there and get that job. May the Lord be with you."*

I got the job.

From Me, to You…

This brief yet powerful encounter is what rekindled my dwindled flame I once had as a young man to gain a personal relationship with Christ and become more in tune with my spirituality. Prior to meeting this elderly parking lot attendant it seemed as if everything I had worked for was falling apart.

Although two years had past, I still dealt with the mental effects of nearly loosing my life, and it seemed as if I just could not pull myself together. I failed to complete a course I needed to remain academically eligible to play football during the summer of 1999. As a result I lost my scholarship. Unable to pay for school on my own I was forced to leave and move back home. Depression began to set in very quickly as I tried to find a job that would do more than simply pay my bills. I felt defeated and worthless. Once again I was almost ready to call it quits. Then that day happened.

In the thirteenth chapter of the book of Hebrews, the writer Paul makes this statement, "Do not forget to entertain strangers, for by so doing some have unwittingly entertained angels." When I pulled into the parking lot the only thing I had to my name was the pocket change he refused to accept. I had never seen this gentleman before in my life, nor have I seen him since. In fact, when I returned back to the lot after my interview, the man was gone. I sat in my car, prayed and gave thanks like I had never done before. And afterward the Lord began to call me time and time again through others.

I dated a young lady who, by a simple invitation to visit her church, connected me to a man who helped to develop and nourish the deep hunger I had inside to know God. Over the years I continued to read and seek answers. Later I was introduced to an individual who was able to help guide me to many of those answers. As time has progressed I have gained wisdom, revelation and understanding of my purpose.

There is a phrase used in the church today called "going through." It is often used to describe the trying times an individual may be going through as a result of "unrighteous living" or suggesting they have done something to offend God. This could not be further from the truth. According to the Apostle Sam Soleyn, The trials we face in our lives from a spiritual standpoint rarely have anything to do with something we may have done. Though it may have the appearance of cause and effect, the eternal implications are much deeper. Our trials are meant to give us the training needed to stand in the day God has called us to walk into, both individually and corporately. Gaining this understanding has taught me how to have joy even through my pain. Because now I know my hardships are not a form of condemnation. And He often reminds us of this truth through others, just as He did with the parking lot attendant.

From Me, to You...

Dear Gran'moan,

I don't even know how to begin this. What do I say to the glue of our family? How can I express the gratitude I have for the love you showed and the laughs you gave us all in this life. There are so many things I remember growing up that warm my heart each time I think of you.

I remember how much you use to travel. It seemed like every month I was asking Momma, "Where's Gran'moan?"

"She's in Chicago visiting Miss Cary... She's in New Orleans at the Mardi gras... She's in Pennsylvania visiting Auntie Li'l Sister... She's in Indiana visiting Auntie Ellen and Auntie Robin."

I tell people today, my Grandma "GOT IT IN!" And no matter where you went, you always brought us something back. There is no doubt Gran'moan loved her babies and she loved her family. And everybody loved you.

Just as often as you would go to visit other people, somebody was always dropping by to see you or spend the weekend with us. Sometimes they stayed the week, whether it was Vince, Miss Cary,

Miss Rose, your sisters, or even our distant second and third cousins. Celebrities like "Fat's" Domino, Levi Stubs from The Four Tops, BB King and Jalen Rose's Mom even came to visit. Oh, and let me not forget the annual Christmas party.

Man… after ya'll came home from the bar on Christmas Eve it seemed like the entire neighborhood was in the house. You would spend days preparing the food. And no matter how many people showed up, there was always enough without having to give them any of the food you made just for the family. I mean you had cold cut trays, cheese and cracker trays, veggie trays, chips and dip, deviled eggs, ham, turkey, greens… you name it and we had it. Well, they had it too (for the party that is). I told Momma and Aunt Diane this past Christmas about how Joel and I knew when it was time to go to bed. It seemed like the minute a particular song came on we had to go. And there was a different one for each type of party.

For the Christmas party, it was "Merry Christmas Baby" by Charles Brown. If the grown folks came over the night of 4th of July it was "Stop Doggin Me Around" by Jackie Wilson. Joel and I got so good at knowing the songs, that when certain melodies or lyrics came on we just headed for the stairs. If we heard… *"Aw Yeah… Shedi-bidi-bi-bi-bee-bee-yeah… Well-ALRIGHT!"* That meant there was a card party. It was either Luther or Marvin when it was time to gamble. No matter the reasons people had or gave, it was just amazing to see how they gravitated to you. No matter what, somebody was coming to check on Gran'moan.

I remember when I was about six I asked you if Mr. Monroe was your boyfriend because he came over the most. You laughed at me so hard, and said, *"No baby, that's just Gran'moan's friend."*

I told Momma that story about a year ago and she laughed just as hard as you did, but she finally told me why my question was so funny.

"Phillip, you don't know who Monroe was?"

From Me, to You...

"No...?"

"Monroe was the number man."

We both started laughing, and I responded, *"How was I supposed to know... I was only six."*

      Looking back, I can see that we didn't always do things according to the rules. But while our family may not have walked a straight line in "everything" we did, none of us set out to hurt anyone and more importantly, I appreciate the fact that you never allowed us to see or even know the darker sides to life as kids. When adults came over to the house you sent us out of the room. When you had to deal with Aunt Jackie, Uncle Kevin or even Uncle John you made us go play. For years I use to think the card parties you threw in the basement were just your friends coming over to eat the chicken you cooked and listen to music. You taught us respect and to know the difference between a child and an adult, sometimes the hard way.

      I remember once when I was about seven I felt the wrath of your hand. As a matter of fact I remember that being one of the last time you had to really put me in my place. I don't recall what I did or what I said. But I do remember talking back to you for something. When I turned and walked down the stairs I thought I was in the clear, especially since I had made it down to the bottom of the steps. Out of nowhere I felt something hit me in the back of the head. It hurt a little bit. But when I saw blood dripping and realized what happened, it seemed like the pain got more intense...

"MOMMAAAAAAAAA!!!!!!! ...AHHHHHHHH... MOMMAAAAAAA!!!!!" I screamed

"WHAT'S WRONG!?"... "WHAT'S WRONG!?" Momma said as she ran to me with concern and fear.

"UUUUUUUAHHHHHH... MY HEAD BLEEDIN'!!!!!!"

"WHAT HAPPEN!?"

"UUUUUAAHHHHH... GRAN'MOAN!!!!!!"

"GRAN'MOAN WHAT!?"

"GRAN'MOAN... UUUAHHHHH..."

"WHAT!?"

"GRAN'MOAN... HIT ME INNA' HEAD WIT' HER SHOOOOOOOOE!!!!!!!!"

By that time, you made it down stairs and must have heard me; because all I heard from around the corner was,

"AND I'LL HIT HIS LITTLE ASS AGAIN... WIT' YO' SMART ASS!"
(Ooh sorry Gran'moan, didn't mean to say that).

I know you felt really bad when you saw that I was bleeding. You just weren't going to apologize.

"Come here baby let me see. Gran'moan didn't mean to hurt you... but next time keep yo' mouth closed and do what I tell you. Hear me?"

We had NO problems after that. Thinking about that story, some people may view that as abuse or going overboard. Which... yeeaaah, I would agree to an extent. It may have been a bit much. But I will tell you...I am not mad at you for it. I can't recall what I did or said, but I know it had to have been out of line. You would never intentionally hurt anyone let alone one of your own.

I see kids today and how they speak to adults, and my heart just falls. They know no boundaries, and have no fear of the consequences of their actions. All it took for us was to hear the words, *"Go get me that switch."* And we got right back in line. I appreciate those lessons, whether they were through calm, but yet stern conversations or when you had to let the belt or switch do the talking; I understood that any discipline you delivered was purely out of love. I know we were better off for them. But I think I learned more by watching you and how you handled situations and people, than I did in any of our sit-downs.

I watched you walk many blocks to the doctor's office when no one had a car. And even when Auntie Diane, Momma, Uncle Richard and Uncle Bobby had cars but not the time to take you; you'd still walk a great distance, in the hot sun to the grocery store to get food for a meal. No matter how bad times got, you made sure we ate. And I don't mean just sandwiches either. I can't begin to list how many different meals you created using leg quarters, fat backs or smoke sausage. How many delicious meals did we have that included some type of rice or green vegetable? No matter what you made sure we didn't miss a meal.

I know how much you loved me, but it wasn't until I got older that I realized how you communicated it. Like how you would always stand up for me. I remember how on the days you cooked shellfish; because of my allergy, I would have a totally separate meal. Most times you would make me a steak because you knew that was my favorite. I'll never forget the time you almost put your hands on Uncle Richard one day for eating a steak that was set aside for me. You were so mad at him.

And what about the time Momma came over to pick me up and we were standing in the kitchen. She started getting on me about how I dressed myself. I'll never forget how you stepped in.

"Girl leave that boy alone. He dresses himself real good. Better than a lot of these kids out here. Hell, better than ya'll use to dress ya'll self in the mornings."

I almost cracked a smile when you walked away until I looked up at Momma. She had a look on her face that said, "I will slap the taste out yo' mouth." But I was still smiling on the inside. I have to say the most memorable moment I have of you coming to my rescue didn't come when someone attempted to do something to me or against me…

One night I was supposed to go out with Alvin, Anthony and the rest of the guys. Now that I think about it, I believe it was either New Years Eve or the 4th of July, because I remember the sounds of big bangs. The 4th of July! That's when it was. I remember…there were fireworks going off too. It wasn't long after you had gone up to bed. Everyone else had already left, and only you, little Lewis, Charles and myself were at home. It was about 10:45, going on 11pm. I came up the stairs to give you a kiss goodnight and let you know I was leaving. But when I kissed you on the cheek and said I'll see you later you, rolled over and just looked at me. Do you remember what you said?

"You going out right now baby?"

"Yes ma'm.."

"Where you goin'?"

"I'm just goin' out wit' Alvin and Anthony-n-nem…"

Then you sat up on the edge of your bed.

"Phillip… baby please be careful out there…"

And as you said it, Grandma… you looked at me with such a look of concern. You didn't say anything else. But…It was as if you were looking at me for the last time.

"I will Gran'moan…"

I kissed you on the cheek and walked away, but as I began to walk down the stairs I looked back over my shoulder and noticed that you hadn't laid back down. You were still sitting up watching me walk down the stairs.

I didn't leave right away. In fact, I sat on the couch for about fifteen minutes, just feeling your spirit speaking to me through that look. You never once, tried to stop me from going anywhere. Judging from the look on your face, it was as if you knew something was going to happen to me that night. So I called Alvin and made up some excuse about me not feeling well. I told him I was going to stay home.

When I walked back up the stairs you were still sitting on the edge of your bed. I didn't know if your back was bothering you, whether or not you had to use the restroom, or if you were planning to go down stairs to get a late snack. But I came back into your room and told you I was going to stay home; you didn't smile or even say much. All you said was, "Ok baby."

And as I looked over my shoulder walking down the stairs, I knew I made the right decision. I saw you laying back down, and getting comfortable under your covers. I truly believe in my heart and spirit to this day; had I walked out of the door something would have happened to me. You always took care of me. It was the little things.

The little things I appreciate now more than ever. The things that didn't seem so significant before, will always be with me, like how everyone in the family would fight over who got to lie in your bed and watch TV when you went downstairs for the afternoon to cook. Joel and I would sprint up the stairs the minute we heard the floor creak. We knew by the sound you were headed down stairs. And as you know it wasn't just us. Whenever Uncle Richard, Aunt Jackie, Uncle John or any adult in the family would come home, they would come right up there and kick us out.

When I spoke about this at the funeral I really didn't have time to think about the significance of it. I don't know why it came to mind. But after I said it, went home and reflected; I realized what it was. It wasn't the fact that your bed was the most comfortable. Though it was.

Nor was it the fact that you had the largest TV in the house. Though you did. And it didn't matter that at some point (sometimes within minutes) you would come back and put us all out yourself. The thing that drew everyone to your room... to lie in your bed... to watch your TV... was you.

I still feel the warmth of your spirit at night, from when I use to lay in your bed. I can smell your perfumes when I close my eyes. I can still feel the security of knowing everything is going to be alright...
"`Because Gran'moan was gone make sure it was alright."

It wasn't until I saw you lying to rest that I realized how many times you said I love you. All the hot water cornbread you made from scratch. The battered fried chicken, the red beans & rice, mashed potatoes, gumbo, stuffed bell pepper... the walks to the grocery store, the times you called me in the house to get your purse off your dresser even though you were laying in the bed less than three feet away from it, the multiple trips to the store to take the bottles back, the candy bars, the lottery numbers, the Faygo Pops, the decks of Aviator and Bumble Bee playing cards... TO THE WAY YOU LOOKED AT ME ON THAT FOURTH OF JULY THAT NIGHT AND SIMPLY SAID...

"Phillip... baby please be careful out there."

Or like the time you stopped Momma from continuing to whoop me in the hallway upstairs.

It's the little things we take for granted, until it is too late, that tells us how much someone loves us.

I love you Gran'moan

"Gran'moan"

by Phil Black

From Me, to You…

It is a known fact that language differs according to race, geography and culture. Depending on who you are, where you are from and what you have been exposed to; we express ourselves differently. Although, we may not speak the same vernacular, we can often communicate our feelings through common, but yet simple gestures.

My Grandmother taught us how to love one another with all that we had and everything we could possibly give, in her own language. By her life and even in her death, I learned the importance of showing others how I feel in addition to telling them. The words I love you are wonderful to hear whenever they are spoken, but the continuous and unfailing display of that notion truly touches ones heart. Whether you are a child or an adult, words may often be misquoted or misinterpreted, but no matter what age you are, the language of consistency is rarely misunderstood.

As a child growing up, my Grandmother, Mother, Aunts and Uncles made sure we had the best Christmases a child could hope for. One year (back when handheld radios were in style), my Mother brought me a boom box with a small black and white television on it. Another year (when Nintendo first launched), she not only got me the game system, but four video games were included. Everything from clothes, bikes, jewelry, toys, and money; though we did not have a lot, they always made sure to save throughout the year for that special day. As a child those things excited me, and I was very happy and appreciative to receive them. But as an adult I realize there was so much more to it.

My best friend tells me how he feels simply by sharing a beer as we talk about our futures. Every time a friend sends me a hello, good morning or note on the Internet it lets me know I am on their mind. Now that I am older my mother and I share our stories of how we interact with others and laugh together over the phone or at a restaurant. And whenever I am feeling down or need direction my Uncle always, has words of wisdom.

Sometimes we miss the messages people deliver, listening or looking for our preferred method of communication, rather than learning theirs. We look for a hug rather than a handshake or a kiss, instead of a caress. And while we yearn to spend every possible moment with our mate, family or close friends; we forget to enjoy the little time they have available that day. One question we need to ask is, What if the moment you are in, is the last one you will ever have together? A person may not be able to give you the world, spend every minute with you, or always express their love, the way that you wish. But that does not mean it is not being shown or expressed. We all have basic needs and desires that should be conveyed and met when possible, because it is our personal language. However, we must also learn to listen and appreciate others as they speak to us in their own way.

My Grandmother did not come to every football game I ever played in. Nor did she ever hear me speak. But she loved me with all that she had and with any and everything she could give. My Gran'moan gave herself.

by Phil Black

"You and I are two different people..." –**Unknown**

Charles,

I have always seen you as more than my cousin. The day your mother brought you home, I promised myself I would teach you everything I knew, so you could be better than me. More importantly, I didn't want anyone to make you feel like I did growing up. So instead of just simply being your cousin I always felt I needed to be a big brother, and in most cases a father figure as you got older. Recently, since you've been in prison, I realized that I never asked you what you wanted to do or who you wanted to become. I just assumed because I played football that you would want to as well.

Do you remember the first year you went out for little league, playing for the Jet's? I think you gave it a solid week before you came to me a said, *"I don't want to go, can I just play with Devin at home?"* I laugh when I think about it now. But I know I wasn't laughing then. I was upset, because all I could think about was how great you could be.

The way I saw it, if I started teaching you what I knew in high school while you were in little league, then taught you college techniques while you were in high school; by the time you became a senior, you would be one of, if not the best player in the State. So when you asked to play the next year I was super excited.

From Me, to You…

We walked to practice together, ran together; we even did drills in the yard at home together. I was always excited, proud and happy to see you play. But I find it hard knowing I never asked you, if you were happy.

Charles, I know you didn't always understand why I dealt with you the way I did. A lot of times I didn't either. I was making it up as I went along. Whether it was a hug to show you I cared or calling the police to teach you a lesson. I know I was difficult to deal with at times. Hell, I still am; but everything I did and said was out of love. I love you like a father loves his child. The idea of you growing up without someone to look up to reminded me of the lack of my own father's presence.

I never meant any harm. And I never meant to push you so hard, where it would lead to us having so much separation before you went in. For years I couldn't help but feel responsible in some way. Seeing you during your last court date was too much to bear. Even though you are a full grown man, when I looked at you, all I saw was my little dude again. But I know you are not. You are Charles M. Black. A Man. And I love you. I can't wait to meet you, again.

Your brother,
Phil

by Phil Black

From Me, to You...

If you are a parent, older sibling, relative or mentor to a young child, I am sure you can relate to the excitement of recognizing the potential they possess. Sometimes the light bulb is turned on the first time we see how fast they can run or even hear them singing their favorite tune. No matter what the case maybe, when we spot talent in a child, many of us do our best to help them make their dreams become a reality. But I realized from my experience with my cousin, sometime the goals we set for our children are actually our own.

Before my cousin ever showed any interest in playing sports I had already created a vision for his future and plotted the road map for which it was to be accomplished. In my mind there was no doubt he would want to become the next greatest athlete and follow in his big cousin's footsteps. Focused on pushing him toward the goal I set, I became almost totally blind to the issues he faced and disregarded the possible desires he may have had for his own life.

Charles dealt with a lot growing up. Some of the issues he faced I could fully relate to and some I could not. Though I always looked to give him the best advice possible, I rarely acknowledged the fact he was having a unique experience. I spoke to him based on where I came from and not where he was. Charles had a lot of anger and resentment bottled inside that I could never seem to help release nor understand. Now that I am older I can honestly say while I heard everything Charles said, I never really listened.

As family, friends and mentors we must listen to our children. We should always maintain the appropriate amount of distance from their situations to provide objectivity and empathy, while getting down to their level, listening to their concerns and in some cases being sympathetic will make for a more balanced relationship. More importantly, when they feel they are being heard, children are more apt to open up and we gain a better sense of who they are and what they want. To some this may seem very basic. But if you deal with people in the manner I dealt with Charles, I would suggest you try another way. There is nothing wrong with wanting more for a person and pushing them toward success. Just be sure that the goal set before them is their own.

From Me, to You...

"The only way to lose, is by not trying."-**Unknown**

Dear Lewis,

What's going on man? We haven't talked in a while. How is everything going out there in Midland? I have been doing well on my end, just working hard to get this book finished. Which is why I am writing you. Initially I was only going to write a brief letter to you but after speaking to my editor and Momma a lot of things came up that I wanted to explain and express to you.

I sit back in amazement sometimes looking at the man you have become. Yet when I think about how you were growing, I am no longer surprised. You have always been an independent and rational thinker. I'll never forget what you said to Joel when you were about eight years old. He got up early one Saturday morning to catch the bus to the Eastern Market, from Grandma's house, which was no short trip. Joel got back home about three hours later and only had a small bag in his hand. When he placed everything on the dining room table, your expression said it all. It was as if you had to know the logic behind this purchase. Not to bring up how you use to stutter, but it did make your question all the more funny. You looked at the bag... then looked at Joel. Looked at the stuff on the table... then looked at me. When your mother (Aunt Jackie) came down the stairs to ask Joel what he brought; you were more than happy to answer for him.

"Heeeee gaga-got up... OUT da bed. Ca-Caught... t-twooo buses. TOOO-Buy, sSSUUUM incense... aaaAAND Auh piece of fruit."

And if that wasn't bad enough you finished it off with...

"Ya-Yoooou could-have... walked. Six Bl-Bl-Bloocks toooo the store. And got aaaAUH APPLE... aaaAAAnd SuuuM Air freshener!"

I still laugh about that to this day. When I told Momma about that she had her own story to tell.

Momma told me about the time she and Grandma took you with them to the grocery store. I believe you were only four or five. As Grandma and Momma were shopping, you kept grabbing candy for them to buy for you but they kept telling you to put it back. So instead of asking for candy you decided to ask for money.

"Tee Tee... can I have aaaaAAUH Dollar?"

"I don't have a dollar Lewis."

Then you went to Grandma, *"Gran'moan... Gran'moan... caaaAAN I have a dollar?"*

"No Lewis, I don't have no dollar..."

Momma said you just stood in the middle of the aisle as they kept pushing the cart. After a few seconds all they heard was...

"DAAAANG! DAAAANG! YALL AINT GOT NOTHIN!?... NOT EVEN NO FOOD STAMPS!?"

Dude you are hilarious. But just as I said, I saw the type of mentality you had at an early age. Which is why I knew you would be successful.

When the family had to move from the house on Eason I realized it would have been difficult for anyone else to take you and Charles in. Although I knew any and everyone would have made provisions, I felt things would be much easier on everyone if you both came to live with me. Even though I was only twenty three years old at the time, I wanted the responsibility. Not to mention the Ypsilanti school district had much more to offer you. In my wildest dreams I couldn't have imagined you growing the way you did. There were only a couple of times I had to take some of the air out of your chest. But I am glad I did. You were always very observant, humble and obedient. With a spirit like that success becomes a bye product.

Lewis I am writing this letter to say, I see you. I see how you not only worked past your speech impediment, with the help of Cousin James, but I also saw how you remained focused even through the rough times we faced. Lewis, you even fought on as you mourned the death of your father. Today YOU stand as the FIRST to graduate from a four year institution. To top that, YOU are part of the first Mock Trial Team to win by a unanimous vote in the history of the NCAA to become National Champions. And if that wasn't enough you earned honors by being named ALL AMERICAN! I am so proud of you. Words cannot express. When you begin the next chapter of your life at Cooley Law School – YESSIR - and times get a little rough, allow yourself to remember and say this… "I did it!" By His grace and with your determination you came this far. There is nothing you can't do unless you stop trying. Always remember, we – your family – did only what comes natural, as far as raising a well rounded young man. Your strides and achievements are your doing, not mine, not your mother's or father's or Joel or Charles, or anyone else. You…and God alone! We just gave you a little push along the way.

I love you brother,

Phil

"Sometimes we don't realize what we have until it is gone."
-Unknown

Dear Veronica,

I hope all is well with you and Jennifer. It's been over a year since we last spoke on the phone. Hard to believe how much has changed in that short time. We went from reconciling a lost friendship after over seven years of separation, to no contact at all. I wrote you another letter a few months ago (I'm not sure if you got it). Although I am assuming you did considering it never came back. I don't blame you for not wanting to respond. But in case you didn't get it I wanted to reiterate the message.

During the time we dated in college I was very selfish and insecure. I use to think I masked it pretty well. However now I realize you could see through my tough act the entire time. And what amazes me most of all, you loved me in spite of it.

You were the first woman in my young adult life that simply and genuinely cared for me from beginning to end. I'll never forget the day you met my mother when she came to visit in Ypsilanti. Do you remember what you told her?

"I LOVE YOUR SON! The first day I saw him on campus from across the parking lot I said I HAVE TO HAVE HIM!"

I was sitting there shaking my head, thinking *"I cannot believe she just said that to my Momma."* But she burst out laughing. The funny thing is, you were her girl from that moment on. She loved the fact that you were fearless in how you felt about me. You didn't hold punches and were comfortable with yourself. You possessed all the qualities I love in a woman, but I took you for granted.

I didn't realize how much I loved you then, until I was faced with the possibility of never being with you. I remember looking at you from across the room one night while you were asleep, thinking to myself, *"I am going to marry that girl"*. But unfortunately it didn't work out that way.

One of the challenges we as men face during our stage of immaturity, is not recognizing a good woman when she is right in front of our eyes. Because we are not ready, we will either let her go or sabotage the relationship. Some men are fortunate enough to recognize the damage our actions or neglect causes in a relatively short amount of time, but in most cases our time of realization is usually too late. The emotional pain inflicted can be withstanding for the woman that has been hurt. So when we have finally reached that age of maturity, we reflect on what could have been, hoping to one day, get a second chance. Yet the reality of it is; we can only hope to be a little better for the next person.

I'm not writing with the expectation of things changing between the two of us. I just really wanted to reach out and apologize from a sincere heart.

I wish you much happiness and success. I know you will make someone very happy. I pray the Lord watches over you and your beautiful daughter. Tell your Mom, Dad and everyone else I said hello. Be blessed.

Phil

From Me, to You...

Self-sabotaging is a characteristic of many people with low self-esteem. We often feel inadequate and undeserving of certain aspects of our life, whether it is a simple compliment, advancement opportunities on our jobs or even the sincere love and admiration of another. As a result, we subconsciously (and sometimes knowingly) do things to redirect the attention, damaging our success and even destroying our relationships. For a long time I did not feel worthy of success or love simply because I had not dealt with the unresolved issues of my past, or the insecurities of my present situations of the time.

I had a tendency of molding my personality to meet the desires of the person I was with. According to comedian Chris Rock from his 1999 HBO special *"Bigger & Blacker"*, the urban community calls it, "showing our representative". We display all the qualities desirable to whom ever we are set on pleasing, failing to acknowledge or reveal our faults, out of the fear of being rejected. Not realizing that with time, it is inevitable that the rest of our true colors, will surface. So in the meantime, we take pride in displaying these realistic, but not consistent, qualities that are appealing to our love interest or mate. For us men, opening car doors with a gentlemen's grace on a first date, knowing that may not always be our norm, or for women, engaging in conversations with a male interest, fully aware that you do not have a clue or interest in the subject of discussion. We naturally put our best foot forward in the onset of meeting someone new. The problem with this for those who are insecure, is the fear of what happens when the honeymoon period is over?

For many years I painted the best picture of myself possible when I met someone I truly admired. More often than not I set such a standard for myself that I became fearful of not maintaining it or having the ability to push beyond it. I would hide my feelings creating the illusion nothing ever bothered me, or insisted on paying for everything knowing I was not in a good position financially. Over and over again my representative would take the lead. But in the back of my mind I knew I was not being completely honest with myself or the person I was dealing with. And then that one inevitable moment arrives, the situation or circumstance that pulls out that truth in you, that truth you have diligently worked at not revealing…Now what?

Now that you have to show or tell this person you do not have it all together, what is next? How will they react when they find out you are living from check to check? Will they still like you if they knew your credit score was in the basement? What will this person do the first time you take off your cape and show them you are not a super hero but a human that has made a lot of mistakes and needs help to correct them? People with high self-esteem say, "Love me or leave me." In a lot of cases, those with low-self esteem simply run to save face. That is what I use to do. Until I gained more confidence in myself, and realized I am enough and while my current situation may at times be less than favorable, it does not define who I am.

When we are preoccupied with keeping a certain image or are mentally held down by our past, we loose site of the fact that there are people in our lives that simply enjoy us for who we are and not what we can offer. As a result, we put our would-be close friends or significant others at distance, building a wall that can seem impossible to tear down. We keep them close enough to reach but too far for them to touch. There has to be a balance between putting your best foot forward and consistently displaying the qualities that make you who you are. Do not allow insecurities of your past or current situation to prevent you from receiving the blessedness that comes from the love of others. We all face hardships and challenging times. If a person is meant for you they will not be deterred by your struggles. By being forthcoming from the start we not only free ourselves from having to keep a false image, but we allow others to make a conscious decision based on real information as to whether they decide to develop a relationship or not. Holding back the pieces of who we are, the good and not so good pieces that make us complete, takes away from others ability to make an honest decision on whether or not they can be apart of our lives. How can one make a sound decision on whether or not they choose to deal with you if they do not have the truth to work with? So the question of "Now What?", no longer has a place and you can allow the relationship to take its' natural progression.

From Me, to You...

"Then Jesus said, 'Father, forgive them, for they do not know what they do." –
Luke 23:34

Dear Jason,

It's been a long time. Whenever I think of you, the first thing that comes to mind is our old singing group as kids, TLC; Tender Loving Care. Do you remember when you, Armon and I performed at the Latin Quarters down on the Boulevard? We couldn't have been any more than ten or eleven.

We were all dressed in our favorite college short sets. You wore the Duke Blue Devils, Armon wore the UNLV Running Rebels and I wore the George Town Hoyas's. I don't recall every song we sang that night, but I do remember how the crowd got excited when we sang "Childhood Love". We were like superstars for at least a week. It seemed like everyone in school wanted to hear us sing after they heard about the performance. That was fun, but even beyond the singing, we really had some good times hanging out together.

Do you remember when we made our own basketball rims?... We nailed a flat piece of plywood to the tree near the alley behind your house for the backboard. Then we knocked the bottom out of a crate and used it as the rim. The only ball we could use was a small rubber one. No one ever really took notice of our make shift basketball rim, maybe it was because of how much fun we had. If nothing else we always had fun, either playing basketball, football, singing, or just chillin on the block. It wasn't until after high school graduation that we started to grow distant.

When I went to school at Eastern Michigan University I really didn't desire to come home that often. I was happy seeing new things and meeting new people. I know that kind of left you alone, especially since you and Armon didn't talk as much. And Anthony going off to Junior College in San Francisco didn't make it any better. I know things couldn't have been going well when you called me that night...

We talked for a long time. Much longer than we had ever spoke on the telephone before. I knew something had to be bothering you when you mentioned that you really wanted to get away and go to school. Not to imply that school was not a good option for you, it's just the fact that I knew you. I didn't want to get too personal so I did like most of us men do; I told myself I would wait until you were ready to talk to me instead of asking. Sometimes I think that if I had inquired that night and allowed you the opportunity to release whatever you were dealing with... you would still be here today.

DAMN JASON!

What was it man!? What could have been so bad!? What could you have been going through that seemed so fuckin' bad!?...What made you shoot yourself IN-THE FUCKIN' HEAD WITH A SHOTGUN!? WHAT!?... Dog we loved you man...

Didn't you know how much we loved you? Man, you were funny... talented... athletic... girls loved to be around you! Your family looked up to you! FUCK!, I LOOKED UP TO YOU! Back then I wished I had your confidence. I wished people respected me the way that they respected you. You were one of a kind man...

Things were never the same after you left us. Everyone changed in some way. Even though we dealt with death before, like when Rich Brown got killed while we were at Liberty when he got hit by the car; it did not have the same feeling as this. Brandon said it best at your funeral…

"I don't know how to deal with the pain and anger I have. In situations where someone kills your family or friend it's easy. You ease the pain by going after the person who did it and get revenge. But today, aint nobody to go after. He did it to himself."

Jason, I was mad at you for a long time man. "Why didn't you say something?" Then I got angry with myself for not asking. Maybe if I had been a better friend and came to see you more, called you more; or even invited you up to campus so you could see more… you would still be here. That is what I carry with me. I just hope and pray that you forgive me for not listening. I love you brother.

Your friend, now and forever,

Care

by Phil Black

From Me, to You…

There is a little fact often discussed and well known among men. Sometimes we share laughs about it as we bond over cold beer letting out frustrations of the previous week. Comedians even use it as material when pointing out the differences between men and women. For ages we have discussed it. To this day most people simply accept it. And while it is one of the most important factors in our development as humans, the fact is, men in most cases do not express or communicate personal matters of the heart well, as a result, we are rarely understood.

In his 2003 stand up performance titled "Killin' Them Softly", comedian Dave Chappelle spoke on this topic. Dave explained the difference in how men and women relate through story telling. He suggested men stick to simple facts while women have the tendency of incorporating their feelings about the situation discussed. I think Dave hit the nail on the head.

Most men shy away from topics that stir up emotions whether it is with a woman or a man. The thought of engaging in dialogue that uncovers our sensitive side is both scary and difficult. The fear of losing respect from others is what prevents us from sharing. While the challenge lies with our inexperience, lack of coaching and the age old myth that communication is simply something real men do not involve themselves in.

For men, our image is one of the most important things we possess. A lot of men are reluctant to share their true feelings with people for sake of compromising their masculinity. We are taught, from the time we are young, boys do not cry. Men face situations, deal with them and keep moving on. Rather than asking, "how do you feel", society says, "get over it". So rather than being honest with ourselves and others, risking the possibility of being seen as "a punk", "soft" or "less than a man"; we bottle those emotions inside and continue to add more layers of tough skin with every painful situation. I have come to realize, it is not a matter of whether or not we want to talk. But rather, who can we talk to.

Most, if not all men desire someone they can confide in. Idealistically we would prefer another male to talk with. Unfortunately finding a positive, capable, accessible and willing male influence can sometimes be difficult (if not impossible) for most men. And then you have those who have been raised without any male influence at all. That alone, can set a standard. Sometimes, if there is no male figure present in the initial development of a young man, then there is a great chance that he may not be prone to revealing his personal thoughts and concerns to other men throughout his progression in life. Because of these barriers with communication, comfort and security within male to male dialogue is often none existent. This failure to discuss and reveal personal matters of the heart, can lead to mental solitary confinement.

When we face troubled times or painful situations, men often escape to the place we feel most protected, our own minds. There we are free from judgment of others and are able to collect ourselves as we search for resolution. Or in some cases we do not search at all. We simply let time pass and in the process, work its healing magic. But we fail to realize, by isolating ourselves from others, only seeking answers within ourselves and sweeping these emotions under the rug, we find limited, if any solutions at all. And when you have been taught, fixing problems and dealing with pain is what a man does, as oppose to healing it, buried pain and suppressed emotions are likely to multiply. This inability to express personal feelings and emotions could lead to some males channeling their emotions through extreme and unproductive ways, and depending on the severity of what is not being revealed, maybe even suicide.

There were a total of 32,637 deaths by suicide reported in 2005, according to the U.S. Suicide Statistics (www.suicide,org). Of those reported, 25,907 were by men; 13.5 percent fell in the range of 15-24 years of age.

This is more of a problem than most people are willing to deal with. No longer can we allow our fears and egos to destroy us from the inside out. It does not make you less of a man to say "I am hurting" or "I need help". You do not have to have all the answers. The time has come for us to walk in truth and deal with the realities of right now. We cannot afford to ignore this problem. If you cannot open up to someone in your immediate family or a close friend, seek counseling from a professional.

If you are in need of help go to www.suicidehotlines.com for a toll free number in your area. Or call 1.800.784.2433

From Me, to You...

"These are clapping dogs, rhythmic dogs, harmonics dogs, house dogs, street dogs..." –Atomic Dog George Clinton

Hey QUUUUUES!

First, I want to say; Ya'll crazy as hell. I don't know what in the world I was thinking about when I first decided I wanted to be part of this organization. Wait... Now I remember...

It was an early Saturday afternoon during the summer of 1987; while clicking through the television stations (yes...clicking). As I turned through the stations looking for one of my favorite shows I happen to come across what seemed to be a competition.

There was a group of girls on a stage doing some sort of dance routine. The show caught my attention immediately. Not because of the steps, the girls were really pretty. It only took a matter of minutes for me to look past them and actually pay attention to what they were doing. The motions they were using resembled cheerleading, only much more intense. Dressed in pink and green they kept making this high pitched noise for some reason every time they finished part of their routine. I didn't really get it, but what the heck; it was either that, or play outside by myself.

I saw a couple more groups go on after them. A female team and a guy group dressed in red and white. Even though everyone was dressed differently and obviously part of a different team, they all seemed to do similar moves. But the guy group did have these red and white canes. They used them in their routine and it actually got me a little excited. I had never seen that before in my life. In one of the steps, they were lined up, one behind the other. Without looking backward the guy in front would throw his cane to the guy at the back of the line. The entire time they stayed in rhythm passing the other canes up like an assembly line. It was pretty cool. But then It happened…

After the red and white team left the stage the program broke for commercial. I ran into the kitchen to get a drink. When I came back the announcer was on the stage. He introduced the last act but I couldn't quite hear their name, before the announcer could even finish speaking, a mob of people barking like dogs drowned him out. I had the feeling that something was going on. Then all of a sudden, when he left the stage all you heard was…

BOOM!...BOOM! …BOOM!...BOOM!

The sound reminded me of a set of bass drums. Only these were not drums at all. They were boots hitting the floor, with force. I felt the rhythm in my chest. Before I knew it, I was all of twelve inches away from the television. One by one, men dressed in white tuxedos decorated with purple bow ties and cummerbunds, took the stage. And as nicely put together as their clothes were, my eyes could not help but to go almost immediately to their feet. There they were… those SOLID GOLD army boots on every one of their feet. Once everyone hit the stage and reached formation, the team stopped in unison…

BOOM!

AHR! AHR! AHR! AHRF!... more barks, screams and applause. Then silence…

148

From Me, to You…

"AHRF!"

One of the guys jumped out of line and marched to the front of the
stage. By this time I am waiting with so much anticipation. Then he
yelled out…

"WHEN I SAY QUE! I WANT THE QUES TO GO EYEEEEE!!!!!!!!!"

The auditorium EXPLODED! People were standing on their feet,
jumping in the air, yelling random names. I can't remember one step
those guys did but all I remember thinking was, "I want those boots".
That was my first time being exposed to the Black Greek Letter society
and the Ques. But it certainly wasn't my last.

My senior year in high school, just after the season was over,
and with graduation only months away; I couldn't wait to get the
opportunity to see what college life was like. Up to that point the
closest example I had was the movie School Daze. And if it was
anything close to that… SIGN ME UP! But I soon got an opportunity to
experience it firsthand…

The University of Michigan's Black Student Union hosted a
weekend visit each spring. Each year they would select three to four
high schools, and invite roughly twenty five students from each school
to stay on campus for the entire weekend, under the supervision of a U
of M student. And in the spring of 1995 Highland Park High School
was one of the four schools selected. When we got the news you
would have thought we won the lotto.

"Dog, it is on!" Nick said with conviction.

"You aint kidding. I can't wait."

We got to the campus at about 6pm on a Friday. As our bus pulled up we saw two of the other buses as well.

"I'm looking for the college freaks!" Anthony blurted out.

"I feel you. We see these babes all the time." I replied. And even though I wanted to meet the women, there was another part of me that was looking to see the overall college life. Which really meant…*"Where are the Que's?"*

After we grabbed our bags and stepped off the bus we were greeted by a hostess. And she was bad! All of the students and most of the chaperones met in the Union hall. They prepped us on why they chose our schools and what they hoped for us to gain from the entire experience. Almost midway through the meeting, the back door opened up and these two guys walked in as if they owned the program. Everyone turned around with eyes fixed on them. They both had on Purple shirts. One had on Camouflage pants and the other ripped up denim shorts, a hat turned backward for one, and a hat cocked to the side for the other. But on their feet was the most amazing site for me. Those Gold Boots!

After the two guys walked in and hugged every female that was part of the program the coordinator continued. At the conclusion of the meeting she asked - for me - the easiest question of the day.

"Who would you all like to stay with for the weekend?" And without hesitation, pause, stutter or blinking of an eye; I stood up and pointed my finger,

"I'm with them!"… The Ques started laughing.

Right after I stood up, Nick and Keith stood up and said the same thing. I happened to look at the program coordinator and her smile of joy changed to a look of concern, *"Gerald…"* she said to one of them. Smiling back at her he said, *"What?"*

"Gerald... don't get these kids drunk!" She must have known something we didn't know. But I couldn't help thinking to myself, *"Kids?... girl do you know what I'd do to you?"*

"Girl I know, relax. We're gonna take care of 'um." Gerald replied.

With that being said, the five of us jumped in Gerald's car and headed for the Que's house. Gerald and Sam were their names. Gerald told us they just crossed the previous year in 1994 and there were a total of seven people on their line.

"On your line, what does that mean?" , I asked with obvious interest,

Gerald replied, *"A line is a group of people trying to enter the organization at the same time."*

Now as I recall, the program director gave the Ques one specific instruction, "Don't get them drunk", but the second we stepped into the house, after introducing us to Mike and Ron he said,

"I'm headed to the store, what ya'll want?" Nick looked at me... I looked at him... *"Two 45oz bottles of Eight Ball!"* And just like that as Nick had previously prophesied, IT WAS ON!

That weekend sealed the deal of my fraternal future. Every aspect of my encounter with the Ques convinced me that they were for me and I was for them. These guys gave and received love from everyone they interacted with, which seemed like the entire campus.

That Saturday, the Ques threw a party on campus! It was packed to capacity. There were enough Ques there to wrap around the entire ballroom; stomping around with vigor and intensity, in a full circle. This was amazing to me. And later that night, while at their Scholar House, I saw a bruh with a vintage checkered, pinstriped sports coat on, with tan and suede elbow patches, and I thought to myself, "these guys are live as ….." Honestly, I thought the out fit was ridiculous, but there was a sense of confident individuality that could not go unnoticed. As refreshing and completely OWT that was, what put the proverbial nail in the coffin for me, was when I saw Brother Calvin hopping around a pool table with a humongous afro wig on and a jacket that bared the name "Stray Dog" on the back. I must say, that is what truly sealed the deal.

Prior to joining our great organization, I didn't understand what set the brothers apart. But now I know; True Friendship. The men of Omega always displayed a genuine love for one another that was revered by all who came into contact with it. The Ques not only demanded respect; they commanded and earned it. Ques earned the respect of their campuses all over the country, not only because they threw the best parties, but the next day you would find them in class as if their night before was not filled with hard partying and overwhelming excitement, you know, the kind of excitement that would keep the typical college student absent from class the next day, in need of some serious restoration. Ques were able to wreck the yard, make time to study, and participate in honorable projects that united the campus. How else would we have attracted men like Charles Drew, Ronald McNair, Jessie Jackson, Michael Jordan, Steve Harvey, Rickie Smiley, Tom Joyner, Shaquille O'Neal and the list goes on, but it wasn't the Greek letter Omega that made them who they are; in contrast, it has always been the men of the organization to make the fraternity what it is. Why did I decide to become a Que?...

Because, the men of character I observed throughout my life were the type of men I wanted to affiliate myself with, not only because of their great accomplishments; but because of the friendship. We need more of that today.

Roo to the Ques,

Dark Gable

From Me, to You…

Those who know me and have spent time with me over the years, recognize how much I love marching (or stepping as other organizations call it). Many times people ask me, how and why do I march with the passion that I do?

For me, marching is not just something you do. It is not just a form of entertainment you use to get people excited and make them interested in your organization. Hopping and singing is the method I have always used to express my love for the organization, it is also the means by which I tell the story of my process.

When I sing songs like…

"Tell me why," I am putting myself back in time and in the space when I really wanted to know the answer to that question.

When we perform the march, *"We are the dogs,"*

I am thinking of how I felt during that time of my process. (Waiting on that paperwork was rough)

While I no longer knock other organizations that use music or theatrics to capture the audience in hopes of winning step shows; I still appreciate and will always simply rely on the trumpet of my voice and the drums of my boots.

"As iron sharpens iron, So a man sharpens the countenance of his friend." – **Proverbs 27:17**

by Phil Black

4 DADD,

It wasn't until the fall of 1996 that I was able to officially make my desire for Que known. Of course I talked about it with select individuals, but for the most part I tried to keep it to myself. After all, you could get into trouble for that type of stuff. At least that is what I was told. I really wanted to pledge my freshman year, but the Fraternity had just passed a mandate to only consider second semester sophomores or higher for acceptance. When I reflect on that rule now – as a matured adult – it worked in my best interest. Who knows what type of chaos I would have caused as a Que, 18 years old and fresh out of high school? Even though I have always been to myself to a degree, being in the center of conversations, speaking my mind and standing in the forefront has never been a problem.

There was only one Que on campus at the time and I was told he didn't cross there. As a matter of fact, I was told to avoid him. As I reflect, I can only assume that the person who told me that obviously didn't know the Ques. There is no such thing as "avoiding" the bruhz. To know one is to know them all. And there is absolutely no way for a person to cross without being seen by everyone in the area.

One day while walking through campus, I made a stop at a dining area called Eastern Eateries. I usually walked past the event boards unless there was something specific I was told to be on the lookout for. However, my eyes were drawn to the board almost

154

instantly when I walked in. It was one of the first purple flyers I had seen posted on campus. The flyer was for a Smoker. That is what they use to call informational meetings for those who were interested in joining an organization. Finally, my big chance!

When I got to the multicultural center that night where the smoker took place, I couldn't help but notice how nervous I was. If they didn't select me I would die. I was born for this. Aside from wanting to wear the colors and earn my own pair of Gold Boots, I did have my question… I wanted to know everything I could about the Ques. I wondered why these men appeared to be so different. What drew people to them? At the same time, what repelled people from them? And what was even more perplexing, was to see the very same people who obviously did not care for the Ques antics, show respect and sometimes admiration for the things they were able to accomplish. But, what I really wanted to know, more than anything, the question that lingered in my mind more than any of my curiosities was, why are they so close? Before I even had an opportunity to get any answers I was stopped at the door.

"*Hey man!*" Someone said just as I touched the door handle.

I turned around, and there was a guy quickly approaching. I was not too sure of who he was. I'd never seen him on campus.

"*Hey man. Where you headed?*" He asked with a sense of concern and urgency.

"*I'm about to go to this meeting in here.*" I replied.

"*For the Ques?*"

"*Yeah.*" Then this guy, whom I had never met before; never even recalled seeing prior to that moment, gave me probably the best advice I had ever received from a stranger.

"Dude, if I were you... I would not go in there with that red shirt on. That is not the move you want to make."

"It's about to start, I don't have time to run to my dorm. The only thing I have on under it is this blue family reunion t-shirt."

"Well that's better than that red shit you got on bro. Trust me. What's your name?"

"Phil."

"I'm Brian."

Who knew, that simple exchange of words would turn out to be the birth of a lifelong friendship? I took Brian's advice and took that red shirt off. I even went a step further. If a red shirt was going to stand between me and becoming a Que, I'll never wear red again. And with that, I threw my shirt in the trash.

There were about twenty guys who showed up. One of them had on a red shirt. He lasted about ten minutes, which was just enough time for the bruhz to take forty five seconds introducing themselves, sparing nine minutes and fifteen seconds to talk about him arriving, dressed that way. I immediately looked over and gave B a grateful thumb's up. The meeting only lasted about forty five minutes. I guess it didn't take long to identify who they felt would be able to hang out.

Though we started with six guys, only four made it through the 111 days, 1 hour, 9 minutes and 23 seconds it took for our paperwork to go through. All I could do was think back to what coach Runn warned me of years ago, "It aint for everybody." He was right. The waiting period for that paperwork to go through was pretty intense. I mean there were nights we stayed up until 5am in the morning wondering when we would get our membership packets. In preparation of signing on the dotted line we got to know each other very well. We met each other's families and friends, stayed over each other's apartments or dorm rooms. We ate together. We met before class, between class and even after class, together. We really wanted to know each other. While we hated the long wait for our damn paperwork to go through, we all appreciated the time it took. I must say, if we didn't have to wait such a long time; we may not have had the same bond we have still to this day. People often ask, if you had to start all over today knowing the "waiting process" would be as long as it was; would you do it again. And I say with sound body and mind, at the age of 32… ABSOLUTELY.

Ike you are still one of the funniest dudes I have ever met. I'll never forget the night we were practicing for our dog show and you kept taking your coat off and putting it back on trying to buy time, or when you got mad at Brian for not telling you what the "manual" setting on the alarm clock meant. You are unique, team; funny, eccentric and scholarly all at the same time. Roo dog.

Kyrie, you and I didn't always see eye to eye. I think it was mostly because we are so much alike. As we have grown in Que and in life, you have proven to be a great friend and true brother to me. I see God doing great things in your life. Keep the faith.

Old school B-dog, I couldn't begin to think of the words, so I'll just say this…"Talkin-bout that Catfish…", Love you brother.

Phil "The Superstar Dog" Black
3-TG-97

From Me, to You...

There are a lot of mixed feelings and opinions about Greek letter organizations and what they stand for. People say everything from, "Joining a fraternity or sorority is the best thing one could do in their college career." To, "Joining the Greek society takes away your individuality and sense of self." I have heard many religious leaders say, "It is idolatry." Up and down the spectrum, people have presented their arguments for and against these secret societies.

My purpose in writing this letter is not to deter your hopes or dreams, nor convince anyone that my chosen way of life is right or wrong. When I decided to join my organization it was for personal reasons. None of which included the desire to gain respect, attract more women or rub elbows with the affluent men of the world. I chose to join my fraternity The Ques, because, from the outside looking in, they displayed an image of true, honest friendship. An image that shines so well because it is in fact, a reality.

During that third of a year waiting process to enter my organization, I was able to bond with other men who have now become very dear and close to me. Without joining this organization we may not have ever crossed paths. Yet because of one common interest, we have created friendships with each other and many more people across the country. My fraternity not only introduced me to new friends but more importantly, it has taught me how to be one.

I have come to realize, much like other topics, that the argument of whether a person should or should not join a Greek letter organization is strictly based on the opinion of the person presenting the argument itself. If you are thinking about joining a fraternity, sorority or any type of organization, I urge you to do your own research and decide for yourself if it is for you. I was attracted to the camaraderie. But these organizations offer so much more, including networking opportunities and service to the community. Take advantage of anything positive to assist you in your walk through life. If joining a fraternity or sorority is something you wish to do, than go for it.

From Me, to You…

*"Take your time…" –**Unknown***

Dear Michelle,

I hope all is well with you, CJ and the rest of the family. I know it has been a while since we last spoke. I did receive your last message, but I wasn't in a position to respond. I wanted to reach out to you with the hopes of giving us both a little more closure to our relationship, how we came to this point, and why the decision made, was the best for both of us.

I'll never forget the first day I saw you, our sophomore year in high school. Your hair was long back then; down past your shoulders. You wore it just how I like to see it on women, straight and simple. You even had your little bangs slightly draped over your eyes. I thought that was the sexiest thing in the world. You had on a fairly large green T-Shirt that hung about mid-thigh, a pair of semi-baggy jeans, with an outer cuff at the bottom. You finished it off with a pair of white low top shell-toe Adidas with green stripes, a pair of lime tinted shades and a small green purse that you carried across your shoulders, and I noticed how the strap laid right in between your breast. Yes… I remember all of that.

I even remember our first date. I was so excited when you said yes that I didn't even think about the fact that I didn't have my license yet. "I can't take this girl out on the bus!" Is all I thought about after you said yes. My mom had just recently brought her 89 Sundance but I knew she wasn't going to let me drive on a permit. Luckily, Joel had his license and she trusted him. Everything was cool, until I tried to impress you by pulling up to get you myself. Joel was actually going to let me do the driving while he sat in the back seat. Of course that went out the window when I rolled up on your curb trying to turn the corner and park. I still appreciate the fact that you didn't totally clown me after seeing that. I did however, breakout into a heavy sweat when ALL of your family decided to step onto the porch to see if I would finally get it. And I did. So what if it was months later.

I had a great time with you that night at the movies. Do you remember what we saw?... "Dragon, The Bruce Lee Story". The entire time we were sitting there I was trying to figure out, *"how can I hold this girl's hand without being too obvious?"* So when you grabbed mine I was really relieved. I was so happy with just being near you. What more could a fifteen year old ask for on a first date? Back then holding a hand was serious business.

During our ride home, we sat in the back together while Joel drove. No one could tell me he wasn't trained on being cool. Not only did he not bother us, he kept the jams playing loud enough for us to hear but not too loud where as we couldn't hear each other. I loved holding you and talking to you the entire way home. I don't even know what we talked about. I do remember the last song that was played before you got out of the car. I tried to sing it to you as it played. *"Let, me hold you tight... if only for one night... Let me keep you near-to ease away your fears... It would be so nice... if only for one night."* I remember thinking, "Man! Luther right on time!" Who knew that song would follow us after that?

Later that night, we stayed up talking on the phone for as long as we could. When my Grandmother made me get off the phone, I had to turn every ringer off in the house so she wouldn't hear you call back. That was funny, and I will never forget it. I hid on the floor in the dining room, with all the lights out, laying under the table, just to keep talking to you. I wanted to stay on the phone forever. We didn't have anything to talk about and the both of us were tired...

"You sleepy?"...

"Naw, you sleepy?"...

"Naw I aint sleepy. I mean, I'm sleepy but I aint sleep doe... you sleepy?"...

"Yeah, I'm sleepy too but I aint sleep doe either."...

"You want to go to sleep?"

"Why? You want to get off the phone wit me?"...

"NAW! I was just sayin that cause you said you was sleepy..."

"I'm sleepy but I aint sleep doe... you sleepy?"

That went on for over a damn hour. Next thing I hear is the phone beeping over and over again after I woke up in the morning.

The funny thing is our relationship grew from just that. Talking. Becoming and remaining friends. Spending time with each other. Having our own agenda, never being concerned with how other people felt about what we had. I remember how girls seemed to take notice of me as soon as they saw you wearing my football jersey to school. How all of the guys made it a point to tell me about what they saw you doing every chance they got. But that still didn't stop us. At least until I began to listen to what some of them had to say.

At the time I still didn't think much of myself. We had a great friendship and relationship, but I still couldn't figure out... why me? Out of all the guys you could have chosen, why me? Without having an answer to that question (in my own mind), I was open to any explanation someone was willing to give. Even if it was, *"She doesn't really like you"*, which is exactly the one I was looking for to validate the insecurities I had about myself. Cheating on you back then had nothing to do with the other person or you not being ready to take that step. I threw away what we had then, simply because I didn't like me. And in my mind, "If I didn't like me, how could you?" Although it hurt for a long time that you broke it off with me, deep down inside, I was more comfortable being alone. No pressure to reveal myself. I really grew up and matured after that. Especially in the thirteen years in which we had no contact after graduation.

I was so shocked when you called my name as I walked out of the mall that day. There you were after all this time. The first real girlfriend I had in high school. One of the longest relationships I ever had without ever being physical. The minute I saw you, my mind went to us sitting in the back seat of my mother's car, and our song playing in my head as I approached you. I was so nervous that I forgot to ask you for your number. But just how you saved me in the movie theater back in '93, you asked me for mine, and we exchanged. Who knew history would repeat its self later that week?

When we decided to go out I had no idea what we would do. I was relieved to hear you had no expectations either. We went downtown and simply walked and talked. From 10:30pm until nearly 1am we talked by the water. After it got too cold to bear, we drove around downtown and talked more. I thought we would end the night once we made it back to my house where your car was parked. I am still amazed at how it felt so natural to stand there talking just a little while longer in my driveway until 5:30 in the morning. Even after it started raining. As you got in the car and drove away I couldn't help but feel as though the night could not have been any better.

It was as if thirteen years became three days. Everything felt right again. I had my friend back, the girl who was excited just to watch me play ball, the girl who never asked for anything other than to be by my side. The girl who expressed her mutual interest in me; not by saying I like you but by simply asking, "You want to carry my books?" The innocence of what we had was restored at that moment. "This is what I had been searching for all these years." With that thought in my mind I felt as if I knew I was ready to erase the past and reclaim what was mine. Which is why asking you to marry me was the next logical step, at least that's how I rationalized it in my mind.

Although I told you I was engaged twice before you, I truly felt this was different. Knowing what I know now, it was exactly the same. While my feelings for you and toward you were genuine, I was subconsciously looking for you (like the other women in my past) to fill the void I had inside. I grew so much from the time we separated to the day I saw you in the parking lot. I really thought I was ready. However, I have learned that I could never have been ready, until I had first learned to love me. I just didn't see that then.

We rushed into the marriage without resolving things within ourselves. My insecurities and inability to identify and express my expectations, while unsuccessfully trying to hear, listen, and understand yours prior to our marriage, set the stage for a failing relationship. If I had done some serious self-inventory, I would have realized neither of us was ready to spend the rest of our lives together. But I thank you and I thank God for what has come out of this.

Through our experience and time together, I have been able to see exactly what others see inside of me. I realize the type of man that I am and have the ability to become. That revelation combined with the many lessons I have learned over the years, has given me the confidence I needed to be who I have been called to be. And I think... no, I know I'm okay.

Michelle I love you. I thank God for you. And wish you, CJ and your entire family the very best. God Bless and keep you.

Always,

Phillip

From Me, to You…

When deciding to take the sacred vows of marriage it is no secret a lot of things must be considered. For example, each person's philosophy with regard to finances, living standards, how to raise children and so on. For many of you, I am sure this goes without saying. But for those of us who like to believe in love at first sight, or often see the potential in others like me, I would like to offer this advice. Get to know the person you are with.

I do believe it is possible to fall for a person in a very short period of time. As spiritual beings we are often connected with one another simply from brief interactions. But it is that same capability of connecting with each other when combined with unresolved issues, which makes us prone to making rash decisions.

When you consider making someone your life long partner, you must allow sufficient time to see if they are right for you. There are many road blocks we encounter throughout life that simply do not and cannot come up in a simple conversation upon meeting someone. While it is impossible to know exactly how your potential mate will respond to every situation even after years of courting, overtime you learn their strengths and weaknesses. Based on this information you can make more of an informed decision on whether or not this person is the one for you. You may not feel this is necessary when involved with some one from your past; a person you already have prior history with.

That was my situation. My ex-wife and I knew each other from high school. During that time we developed a wonderful relationship. However, over thirteen years had gone by between then and the time we reunited. We failed to acknowledge that those thirteen years were times of experience and growth – essentially, change. The mistake I made was falling in love with the person I use to know rather than the woman she had become. Failing to allow ourselves the needed time to learn one another again, put us both in compromising positions and opened the door for a lot of miscommunication and conflict.

Before you make the decision to follow your heart rather than your mind, ask yourself the following questions, "Am I honestly ready?" "Do I truly know this person?" and "Am I willing to place their needs before my own?" If you as well as your mate can sincerely answer those questions with a yes, then that is all the more reason why you should take your time to be certain. God bless you.

by Phil Black

Dear Donny Hathaway,

Words cannot describe how your music speaks to me. It is as if each and every lyric was pulled from the pages of my heart. While I may not have experienced everything you have sung about, I can relate. I enjoy them all, from, "Little Ghetto boy" to "Giving up", from "A song for you" to "This Christmas". But as much as I love all of your music these words touch me the most:

For all we know,
We may never meet again.
Before you go,
Make this moment sweet again.

We won't say goodnight,
Until the last minute.
I will hold out my hand,
And my heart will be in it.

For all we know,
This may only be a dream.
We come and we go,
Like the ripples of a stream.

So love me…

Love me tonight.

Tomorrow was made for some,
Tomorrow may never come.

For all we know…

From Me, to You...

When I find my true love, If God is willing - and with the help of a few voice lessons - I will serenade her with this song as I propose. It is simply beautiful. Although you are no longer with us, your words and melodies will always live. Thank you Donny, for allowing us to experience the love and beauty of your gift.

Phil

Dear Mr. BB King and Mr. Bobby "Blue" Bland,

I chose to write one letter to the two of you, because I see you both as one in the same. Though both of you have your own individual styles, unique voices, and have built two very successful separate careers for yourselves; when I hear you two sing together on a record your voices sound so perfectly knit, that it would be a shame to try and separate them.

But it isn't just the music the two of you have shared that I have admired over the years. It is the seamless bond of friendship that you guys have allowed the world to witness throughout time. I had the pleasure of seeing you both perform at the Fox Theatre in Detroit back in 1999 (if I'm not mistaken). Before then, I had only heard your music, when my Grandma played your albums, or while catching a tune on the radio. I was able to take my Mom to the concert, as a Christmas present. We had a ball.

Mr. Bobby you came on first. And you had those women in the audience just SCREAMING? I remember thinking to myself, *"These old cats got it goin on!"* Especially when you sang *"It's My Own Fault Baby... Treat me the waaaay you want-to-dooo..."* I was in shock to see my own Mother right there with the fanatic crowd. Then Mr. BB joined you on the stage.

Mr. BB you came out the only way you do best; rolling with Miss Lucille. *"Heeey EVERYBODY... Let's have some fun. You only live once, and when you're dead-you're done.... So Let the Good Times Roll!"* Man! I can still feel the energy. Every time I put on one of you guy's CD's I go right back to that night. My new thing now, is purchasing a lot of the songs that the two of sang together from the Internet so I can play them on my phone or even in my car via Bluetooth through my radio and speakers. But enough of me rambling.

I just want to say thank you for allowing myself and everyone else to see an example of true friendship. Not just friendship in general, but a genuine relationship of love, appreciation, admiration and respect between two men. I have my own partner in crime. His name is

170

From Me, to You…

Brian Jackson. I wish I could say he shared my enthusiasm for your work and the blues in general. But he's still a good guy. Thank you again for everything.

PS

Mr. BB, I had a chance to see you once and even had a meal at your restaurant in Nashville. The food was great but the entertainment was better. And Mr. Bobby, I'm workin' on that growl. Love you guys.

Phil

Dear Bernie Mac,

You have no idea who I am. We've never met before; in person or otherwise. I first saw you perform (as many others across the country did) the first time you appeared on Def Comedy Jam. From the moment I heard your voice I couldn't stop laughing. You opened with the now *famous "I aaAINT Scared-of-you-MuthaFuckas!"* (Laughing right now) I think my favorite part was when you said, *"Sex aint nothin but fifty pumps... count it if you aint got nothing better to do."*

From there I began to follow your career path, from "House Party III" to "Players Club". I even remember your role in "Above the Rim" when you cursed out 2Pac on the basketball court. *"Fuck you Birdie... you ol pickle head Mutha Fucka!"* Now that I think about it. You used that phase a lot waaay before kings of comedy. But I agree, it does sometimes add just the right seasoning you need on the meat of a conversation. *"Seen that Mutha-Fucka-Bobbie...?"* After my friends found out I could imitate your voice, every time there was a get together I became you. As a matter fact, I have been nicknamed the "Stone Bernie Mac" at a local bar my friend and I frequent in Detroit. I am sure you heard it all the time, but your style of comedy was not only unique, but the laughter it pulled from people, like me, often served as therapy.

You indirectly inspired me to not only be real with myself, but over time, you reminded me that it was ok to be myself around others. I wish I had the opportunity to see you perform live before the Lord called you home. But I find comfort in my heart knowing your spirit reached me and many others, and still lives on. *"I'm out Dis-Mutha-Fucka!"*

Your fan, friend and brother,

The Stone Bernie Mac

From Me, to You…

Dear Mr. Dennis Kimbro,

First I want you to know I have all of your books, *"Daily Motivation"*, *"What Keeps Me Standing"*, *"What Makes the Great, Great"* and *"Think and Grow Rich, a Black Choice"*. (If I missed any please write back to let me know so I can get them). I am writing you for two reasons, first, to tell you how your words have influenced my life, and secondly, to tell you that I understand.

In the fall of 1996, I was a sophomore attending Eastern Michigan University. One day my best friend Brian gave me a copy of *"Think and Grow Rich, a Black Choice."* He received it from a business partner of his. He said, *"Everyone that is anyone in business, has read this book and swears by it."* That was enough for me. At the time, I was not the avid reader I have grown to be. In fact, your book was only the second I read from cover to cover at that point. You caught me from the very beginning. The "Acres of Diamonds" story really touched home for me. I was still in the "job hoping" phase of my life looking for anything I was good at, that I also enjoyed doing. It wasn't until I got into 'direct sales' that I stopped moving from place to place. Your books gave me a lot of the mental food I needed to understand the importance of sticking with it, never giving up, and pressing forward. *"What Makes the Great, Great"* is the book that really took me over the top. So thank you for being an inspiration.

As far as what I said about understanding; I mentioned my best friend Brian? Well he came to Clark Atlanta on a college tour with his students about five years ago. Before he left, Brian vowed to find you wherever you were on that campus. And he did. I am sure you don't remember this, but he called me from your office and gave you the phone. I was really excited to get the opportunity to speak to you. But the excitement faded for a moment when I caught your tone.

I guess I was expecting you to be just as excited to speak to me as I was to speak to you. However, as soon as we ended our five second conversation; I realized that even role models get tired. I pictured you having a rough day of meetings, and students looking for extra leniency on their grades. So after I reasoned with myself, I felt better, so even more now than ever, I want you to know, I do understand.

Be Blessed and Encouraged,

Phil

From Me, to You…

"A person must have three qualities to be considered a leader. Desire, Work Ethic and Commitment. All three must be present or else it or they will not work." –**Steve Carter**

Dear Mr. Zig Ziglar,

I was first introduced to you when I entered the world of network marketing, in late 2002, early 2003. The first audio recording I ever heard was *"Sell your way to the top."* I loved the way you told stories. As a matter of fact, I think I got caught up in the heavy Southern accent like everyone else. But from that point on, I made it a point to get my hands on any and every book or CD of yours I could find. And I think I got a nice amount. *"'A View From The Top', 'Five steps to Successful Selling', 'The Art of Closing the Sale',' Self Image', 'Goals', 'Top Performance',' Staying Up, Up, Up in a Down, Down World'…"* anytime I saw something new of yours, and I had the money, I bought it.

I totally credit most, if not all of my sales success to you. Studying and learning your techniques helped me to experience a significant amount of success while I was involved in network marketing. But it wasn't until I entered the field of direct sales back in 2004 that I really had the opportunity to test the skills I learned.

I started working for a company called The Phone Solution on November 8, 2004, prior to that; I was working as the logistics manager for a top retail store in Ann Arbor Michigan. I was making pretty good money. Working third shift and being a key holder took me to $17.50

an hour. I was twenty seven at the time. One day I went to the mall to fill out applications for a part-time seasonal position. I just wanted to make some extra money for the holidays. When I got there I ran into one of the elders of my former church. He explained that he was a Regional Sales manager for the largest mall based wireless company in the country. He was there interviewing people for sales reps. what I didn't know at the time was the fact that there was only one person currently working there, and he had put in his two week's notice.

Travis continued on to say he was also looking for a manager to run the location and asked if I would be interested. I said, *"I don't need a management position. But if the money is right, I always keep my options open."* To make a long story short, the amount of money at the time wasn't close to what I was currently making. But I decided to join as a part-time sales rep because of the opportunity. Plus, I always wanted to see how well I could do in direct sales.

I started training on Monday November 8th. It took roughly two hours of information for me to make a decision. Not that my trainer did an incredible job of delivering the information. As a matter of fact she was terminated about two weeks later. I could see through her that the opportunity was available, and I actually visualized myself standing in front of that same room doing what she was doing.

That night, without having had any prior direct sales experience; I put in my two week's notice. My friends and family thought I was crazy. I may have been at the time. But I remembered from one of your audio recordings, you said, *"If you are going to be in the profession of selling, get in. If you are going to be out, GET OUT!"* Obviously I took that to heart. I realized, for me to give myself a true genuine shot at being "one of the great ones" (as you put it); I had to be totally focused. Well Mr. Ziglar, I am happy to say that turned out to be one of the best decisions I ever made in my life.

My first thirty five days as a sales rep I sold a total of eighty two contracts. Based on the way we weighed the sales, my total was sixty seven. I beat the new hire record for the state of Michigan by more than ten. I was then promoted to assistant store manager. For the next sixty days I maintained that average of more than eighty gross contracts. That earned me the Store Manager position by February 1st of 2005. During that month, the training department created a new position called a field trainer. I was offered and accepted the position before the end of that month. April 1st of 2005 I was promoted to the market trainer, where I was responsible for developing and conducting sales, management, and leadership training that was specific to the market's needs. Many of which were launched Nationwide. In February of 2006 I was promoted to National Sales Trainer for the South East Region of the US. I managed the largest training team and territory of our company; a total of 21 Trainers in 16 States/Markets. Mr. Ziglar, if you have been counting, that was five promotions in less than sixteen months. My final move came in September of 2007 when the company moved me back to Detroit to take over as the Sales Market Director for the State.

Please understand, in no way am I sharing this story with you, as if to say there is anything extraordinary about me. But on the contrary, there is something special about you and how you taught me all the way from Dallas Texas. I attribute a large part of my business success to the day I fully understood and adopted your life's philosophy...

"You can have everything in life you want, if you will help enough other people get what they want."

Thanks Zig,

Phil

To My Family:

Angie,

I simply want to thank you for caring. I know we didn't have the best relationship growing up; mostly because I use to get on your nerves so much as a child. Yet as adults, I feel we have more of a sibling relationship than cousins. I don't know when it started, perhaps the qualities have always been there and I didn't take notice; but you have become the care giver for the entire family. If anyone needs you, Angie is there. I especially love the way you have taken it upon yourself to maintain consistent contact with Charles. You truly are an angel. But I'm still mad you wouldn't let me come into the basement when your mother Auntie Diane threw your sweet 16 party.

Love you sis

Joel,

Man I am so proud of you. While everyone (including me) thought you simply didn't care to deal with the family, you were perfecting your craft and working to make a better way for us all. Your music is and will serve as inspiration for our future leaders. Stay in the lab, we'll be there soon.

Love

Angel,

Just like Lewis, you are the second oldest of the next generation. You have fought many battles and won. As long as you keep that same level of determination you will continue to move forward.

From Me, to You...

Cassey,

I use to be very impressed with your skills on the court, but now I am amazed by your academic triumphs. One day soon, I will be able to say (between you and Angel) we have two doctors in our family. I'm proud of you.

Richard Jr.,

You can do whatever you choose. But you have to choose. I can't wait to see you shine.

Ce-Ce,

You are growing. Continue to listen. And keep that joyful personality.

Ivan,

You have more raw talent and natural ability than any of us had at your age. Be confident in that. There is no shame in being the best. Those who are great bring greatness out of others.

MJ,

Why you so quiet?....

Marla,

June 3rd! I know you are really young now, but I can see you making a great impact and contribution to our family and society.

Nikki,

My lil sister… You have such a fun personality and a lot of talent. As you transition into this next phase of your life, humility is going to play a larger role. Team first.

MJ (part II),

….Just kidding before. I love you man. I know I wasn't involved or around a lot as you all were growing up, but watching from a far I can see how mature you have become. You worked really hard to get better in basketball. I remember for a while you were just tall…. However, you kept at it and earned yourself a scholarship. I know it has been a major test for you but just like you fought to get to this level, you can fight to get to the next. If that is what you want. Love you.

PS
Seriously, why are you so quiet?

Allison,

The baby doll of the family. Soon you will be a mother. I can only imagine what you may be feeling inside. It has to be a bit scary. I want you to find comfort in knowing the entire family is here for you. And you have a GREAT man in Uncle Bobby right there with you. But then again you already knew that.

From Me, to You...

Dear T,

I am not sure if you will ever have the opportunity to read my book, nor this letter contained within it. What you did to me as a child was monstrous, cowardly and unthinkable. The idea of you being on the streets, and having an opportunity to take another child's innocence away saddens me.

I trusted you. I looked up to you. For the short time we spent together, I called you my friend. My cousin. If anyone were to ask me, I even thought you would protect me. But you didn't. You took away my manhood before I even knew the definition of a man. You changed the bright colors of hope and happiness I had, into lifeless, dismal shades of shame and uncertainty.

I often wondered who I could have been. Who would I have become? How much more confident would I have been through my younger years, had I simply gone back out to play? How would the situation have turned out if I just knew what it meant to go with my gut?

The sad thing is... I don't know. I'll never know. But what I do know is this; what the devil meant for evil, God used for His good. Satan used you as a vessel to break me before I even had a chance to be built. BUT GOD KNEW!!!!

Though "I know" it hurt Him to see me suffer the shame; just like my other trials, He understood the greater need for His plan. So, is this a letter of hate toward you? In no way! I am even smiling as I write this. The spirits of fear, degradation, anger and revenge no longer have a place with me. I forgive you. And I pray that God has mercy on your soul.

Get some help.

And seek the Lord.

Be blessed

From Me, to You…

In the commentary subsequent to my letter to Uncle John I spoke about dealing with the issue of being sexually assaulted from a practical and more so mental standpoint. Now I would like to give both the mental and the spiritual perspectives, of how I viewed and overcame that moment in my life.

Some religions teach God's desire is for us to love our fellow man and forgive them of their sins against us. Yet often times this message is given without providing direction or insight into our personal circumstances, leaving us with that unanswered question; "Why should I let go of the anger I have toward someone who did me harm?" Or as the bible puts it, "How can I forgive a man of his trespasses … when the deed they committed is so unforgettable?"

When we hold on to the offenses of others, which have been inflicted on us, we sometimes create a mental defense mechanism in our minds with the hopes of it resolving the pain that we feel. Most often when the victims in these types of offense are our youth, protection and comfort usually takes precedent over revenge. In that time, we try to distance ourselves from the very person and situation, which caused the pain, through means of physical distance and avoidance from communication. We later realize that these methods do not provide a resolution, nor do they free us of the pain.

On the contrary we become prisoners to our unanswered questions, fears and unexpressed emotions. Keep in mind forgiving someone does not entail giving them an eternal pass to commit the same offense. However, by releasing those feelings and asking the questions, you allow yourself to move forward in your own life. I have found much liberty in sharing my past, realizing I am not the only one in this world who has been violated or hurt by someone. More importantly, through seeking answers to the questions, I have an acceptable answer as to why it all happened.

From Me, to You…

Forgiving my assailant had nothing to do with him as an individual. But rather it has everything to do with my relationship with God, the recognition of His calling on my life, and understanding the power of His forgiveness. When you truly forgive others it releases a feeling within your spirit that is almost indescribable. It is as if you are truly being set free. God does not want us to be held captive and in bondage to our enemy through the experience we dealt with. We must deal with the emotions we have and release our anger and disappointment. By doing this we disarm our spiritual enemy and break the chains of condemnation as we live in freedom.

by Phil Black

*"Sometimes the only way to change the people around you is to change the people around you." –**Unknown***

To the ones who dare to be themselves,

I have come to realize, being an individual is one of the most difficult things in life for one to be. Although, the world is made of people from all walks of life varying in speech, appearance and personal preferences; we tend to categorize and often alienate those who do not fit the general mode. Whether it is the clothes we may wear or the activities we choose to involve ourselves in. If you dare to walk your own path, the world just may label you as strange.

When playing football I prided myself on doing things the right way, all of the time. If we had to run I made sure I didn't cut corners. During drills I was sure to be first. If the coach asked for volunteers I raised my hand. From that I began to notice just how many people did the opposite. The vast majority of the people around me were happy doing things half speed. They did not see exercise as a way of improving themselves and ultimately improving the team. They saw it as extra work. So when eighty percent of the individuals you encounter have the same mindset, being yourself can cause major issues.

Being an individual poses a threat to those who are content with the status quo. In elementary school we refrain from answering or asking questions for fear of judgment. In high school we skip classes or cause disruptions because everyone else is doing it. As adults we purposely hold our opinions knowing our colleague or superior has it all wrong. No one likes to be labeled as strange or different. Yet without those who dare to carve their own path we would be subject to mediocrity and a bland lifeless world lacking creativity.

I could be wrong, but some may have called Erykah Badu "different" when she decided to change the spelling of her name and wear the fabrics of our African heritage. But today she is recognized as one of the most profound and innovative artists in history. I guess that is different. I can imagine a group of kids approaching a young LeBron James on the basketball court, while practicing alone trying to convince him to hang with them instead of working on his shot. "Strangely" enough he decided to stay. And I imagine what the expressions are like now on the faces of those who smirked at a child named Barack when he first said the words, "I want to be President."

Some of the greatest athletes, scholars, community leaders, teachers and parents where all labeled as being "different" at some point in their lives. I have come to realize, when we are bold enough to stand out, we often provide courage for others to stand up. Whether you are a child, young adult, high school student, parent, professional, or like me, an average ordinary individual who happens to have above average hopes, dreams and desires; it is not only your right to be different, it is your calling! Do not allow those who were not given the gift of your vision to hinder you from accomplishing the thing you have been called to do. Most people are unable to see your vision because it was not meant to be seen, until you brought it forth. So for those of you who dare to be individuals, by all means; Be strange. Be bold. Be different. Be you, and do so gracefully.

by Phil Black

Life Lessons

I would first like to say thank you. Thank you for taking time out of your daily life so I may share my experiences with you. For those of you who know me, thank you for taking the chance at getting to know me better. And for those of you who I may not know and may never get the opportunity to meet face to face, we now have a connection. It has always been a personal goal of mine to make anyone I have connected with a little better off than they were before they met me.

So my first message to you is; it is okay. While you may be going through some type of trial and or struggle that may be new for you; know that, it is routine for God. He has an eternal purpose for you and your life that will not fail to be accomplished. Your only job in the deal is to believe. He will do the rest.

Secondly forgive yourself; for anything you may have done or for what may have been done to you. Often times we mentally beat ourselves continuously for the same offences, reliving them time and time again. We must understand while these events helped define who we are, they do not determine who we shall become. Learn to see things from an eternal prospective rather than, the here and now. It will enable you to identify how each trial and triumph is linked to your destiny.

To the insecure; work diligently to identify where your unhappiness truly lies. Once you honestly recognize your issues, then you can work on eliminating them. It is the only way you will be able to move forward in your life with an understanding of your greatness, and with any hope of having healthy relationships. I know firsthand the damage that can be caused if you don't. I have self sabotaged many good relationships because I had unresolved issues. And having been a severely insecure person, my message is this; only you, can decide to overcome and heal. And for the ones who truly care; No matter how much you push, pull, pamper and cheer for an insecure person, they will never become the person they are destined to be until they deal

186

with their own issues face to face. They will continue to misdirect their anger, hurt and or resentment toward others until they are forced to look in the mirror. Trust me I know.

To the seemingly unloved; I challenge you to go out and spread love. I heard Zig Ziglar say once, *"If you go out looking for friends you may never find one, but if you go out to be a friend you will find them everywhere."* The funny thing about love is that it always has a tendency to come back to you. But if you never give it, how can you ever expect to receive it? But this starts with you first. Learn to treat yourself well and it will become easier to treat others well. Those who love themselves realize that it does not take away from them, to love another. In contrast it adds to who you are.

I may be an idealist, but I truly feel the world would be a much better place if we had a better understanding of the simplicity of God's plan and purpose. I know I have become better within myself. It is true. There is liberty in Christ. And He does reward those who diligently seek Him. But the question is, what is that reward? It certainly isn't money, nor is it earthly possessions. It is Love, Peace and Joy. I am happier today than I have ever been in my life. I am at peace with all that I have gone through. I have forgiven those who have sinned against me. I would even love to stand face to face with them all again one day, because they helped me become who I am. And I think I turned out okay.

Lastly, if you have not figured out what this book is truly about, than I leave you with these words:

"My command is this: Love each other as I have loved you. Greater love has no one than this, that he lay down his life for his friends."-John 15:13

So…

"Dear friends, do not be surprised at the painful trials you are suffering, as though something strange were happening to you. But rejoice that you

participate in the sufferings of Christ, so that you may be overjoyed when his glory is revealed. If you are insulted because of the name of Christ, then you are also blessed, for the Spirit of glory and of God rests on you." -1 Peter 4:12-14

Therefore…

"I beseech you, brethren, by the mercies of God, that you present your bodies a living sacrifice, holy; acceptable to God, which is your reasonable service."-Romans 12:1

In other words, this is my life… From Me, to You…

LEARN-LIVE-LOVE

From Me, to You…

Acknowledgements

To My Angels at Rest
Our time together here was like the blink of an eye, yet the impact you have made will carry on forever. I will see you in time.

To My Family,
Thank you for your love and support through this process. I love you all with every part of me.

To My Friends,
I cannot thank you enough for the encouraging words and inspiration you have given me over the years. From the time I posted the idea of writing a book you all have shown me great love in person and online.

To my Editor,
Tara, you are very gifted. I knew you could do it. I cannot wait for you to see what God has for you.

To My Editing Team (Friends),
Mia, Toya, Kianga, Joe, Schranda, Mr. Bradford and Keith, thank you all for your honesty and making yourselves available. This could not have happened without you.

Special thanks to,
Mr. Antwone Fisher, thank you for responding. I have also recently purchased your book of poetry, "Who Will Cry for the Little Boy?" (Published by Mr. William Morrow) And of course it is excellent. I wish you much continued success.

Suggested Readings

By Dennis Kimbro

Think and Grow Rich a Black Choice

Daily Motivations FOR African-American Success

What keeps Me Standing

What Makes the Great, Great?

By Zig Ziglar

Goals

A View from the Top

5 Steps to Successful Selling

Sell Your Way to the Top

Top Performance

The Art of Closing the Sale

Staying Up, Up, Up in a Down, Down World

Self Image

Conversations with my Dog

By Steven Covey

7 Habits of Highly Effective People

The 8th Habit

By Ken Blanchard & Spencer Johnson

The One Minute Manager

The On Time On Target Manager

By Anthony Robbins

Giant Steps

Unlimited Power

By TD Jakes

5 Steps to a Turn Around

Man Power

He-Motions

From Me, to You…

Into the Hearts of Men
Command the Officers

By MLK Jr
A Knock at Midnight
I've Been to the Mountaintop

How to Be a People Magnet, **by Leil Lowndes**
Building Wealth, **by Russ Whitney**
Execution, **by Larry Bossidy & Ram Charan**

By John C. Maxwell
Thinking for a Change
Today Matters
21 Irrefutable Laws of Leadership
Failing Forward
Leadership 101
Equipping 101
Attitude 101
Ethics 101
Developing the Leader With In You
Developing the Leader's Around You

Who Moved My Cheese, **by Spencer Johnson**
The Richest Man in Babylon, by **George S. Clason**
Jesus Life Coach, **by Laurie Beth Jones**
The Power of Positive Thinking, **Dr. Norman Vincent Peale**
Network Market –**Jim Rohn**

By Antwone Quenton Fisher
Finding Fish
Who Will Cry for the Little Boy?

The Bible

Works Cited

"If", a poem by Rudyard Kipling - "Who Will Cry for the Little Boy", by Antwone Fisher, published by William Morrow – "After a While", by Veronica A. Shoffstall – "Killin' Them Softly" HBO special performed by Dave Chappelle 2003 – "Bigger & Blacker" HBO special performed by Chris Rock 1999 – "BET Comic View Special" performed by Cedric "The Entertainer" 1992 – "Fresh Prince of Bel-Air" by Andy Borowitz and Susan Borowitz, produced by NBC productions, the Stuffed Dog company and Warner Bros. Television 1990 – "Full House" by Jeff Franklin, produced by Jeff Franklin, Thomas L. Miller, Robert L. Boyett 1987 – "Dragon, The Bruce Lee Story" written by Rob Cohen and John Raffo, produced by Raffella de Laurentiis, directed by Rob Cohen – "School Daze" written by Spike Lee, produced by Grace Blake, Loretha C. jones, Spike Lee and Monty Ross, directed by Spike Lee – "House Party 3" written by David Toney, Takashi Bufford, characters by Reginald Hudlin, directed by Eric Meza, produced by Carl Craig, Cindy Hornickel, Doug Mchenry, George Jackson, Helena Echegoyen, Janet Grillo – "The Players' Club" written and directed by Ice Cube – "The Original Kings of Comedy" written by Steve Harvey, D.L. Hughley, Cedric the Entertainer and Bernie Mac, produced by Spike Lee, Walter Latham and Davis M. Gale, Directed by Spike Lee - "Dear Mamma" by Tupac Shakur, J. Sample, T. Pizarro, produced by T. Pizarro, DF Master Tee and Moses 1995 – "For All We Know" by Donny Hathaway – "Bad boy/Having a Party" by Luther Vandross, written by Sam Cooke, Marcus Miller and Luther Vandross – "Doggin' Around" by Jackie Wilson, written by Paul Tamopol, Produced by Dick Jacobs – "Merry Christmas, Baby" by Charles Brown, written by Lou Baxter, Johnny Moore – "Into the Hearts of Men" by TD Jakes – "Come On, People" by Bill Cosby and Alvin F. Poussaint M.D., published by Thomas Nelson 2007 – "Finding Fish, a memoir" by Antwone Fisher, published by William Morrow -U.S. Suicide Statistics, www.suicidestatistics.com – Sam Soleyn, www.soleyn.com - "Bible"

From Me, to You...
By Phillip Mozelle Black